Yuupurnju: A Warlpiri Song Cycle

Sung by Henry Cooke Anderson Jakamarra

With transcription and interpretation by
Jerry Patrick Jangala, Steven Dixon Japanangka,
Wanta Steven Patrick Pawu-Kurlpurlurnu Jampijinpa,
Carmel O'Shannessy and Myfany Turpin

The designs, songs and stories in this book are owned by the Warlpiri people of the Northern Territory, Australia. This book has been made to help Warlpiri people maintain the Yuupurnju ceremony and for non-Warlpiri people to learn about Warlpiri language, music and culture. The creation of this book has followed the cultural protocols of prior informed consent, attribution to traditional Aboriginal people and communities, cultural integrity and the sharing of benefits. It has been published with their consent, and the consent of their descendants. Using this knowledge for any purpose that has not been authorised by Warlpiri people may breach the customary laws of Warlpiri people and may also breach copyright and moral rights under the *Copyright Act 1968* (Australian Commonwealth). Please contact the publisher for further details.

First published by Sydney University Press 2024
© Cultural knowledge Warlpiri people
© Audio Henry Anderson Cooke Jakamarra
© Hand drawings of women dancing Carmel O'Shannessy
© Song transcriptions Myfany Turpin
Copyright of graphics as per individual attributions
© Sydney University Press 2024

Reproduction and Communication for other purposes
Except as permitted under the Australian *Copyright Act 1968*, no part of this edition may be reproduced, stored in a retrieval system, or communicated in any form or by any means without prior written permission. All requests for reproduction or communication should be made to Sydney University Press at the address below:

Sydney University Press
Fisher Library F03
Gadigal Country
University of Sydney NSW 2006
AUSTRALIA
sup.info@sydney.edu.au
sydneyuniversitypress.com.au

A catalogue record for this book is available from the National Library of Australia.

We acknowledge all First Nations Australian people who have passed on their culture through generations and continue to do so into the future.

ISBN 9781743329481 paperback
ISBN 9781743329573 epub
ISBN 9781743329603 pdf

Cover image: *Women's Dreaming* © Judy Nampiya Martin Napangardi/Copyright Agency, 2022
Cover design: Nathan Grice

We acknowledge the traditional owners of the lands on which Sydney University Press is located, the Gadigal people of the Eora Nation, and we pay our respects to the knowledge embedded forever within the Aboriginal Custodianship of Country.

Cultural safety

Aboriginal and Torres Strait Islander readers are advised this publication contains names and images of people who have died. The inclusion of any names, voices and/or images of deceased people is done with the permission of their family.

This book is dedicated to Warlpiri people, especially those who have been learning and teaching traditional songs for many years.

Contents

Preface	ix
Forewords	xi
List of contributors	xv
Acknowledgements	xxiii
Introduction to Warlpiri song cycles	1
1. Kanaku kanakurla	17
2. Karrinjapardi	19
3. Tangkirrina	21
4. Wujuju-wangkanya	23
5. Yajankurlarri	25
6. Yanganpa	27
7. Yarrintilarnu	29
8. Jinapi	31
9. Miyinmarrirla	33
10. Manja kurrkurrku	35
11. Jujuju japarnti	37
12. Walangkaju	39
13. Palararrararra	41
14. Kartiwirntinya	43
15. Warrawarra	45
16. Yuluwurru	47
17. Yangipi yantakuyanta	49
18. Karnta wurrparna	51
19. Waku mirntirrirla	53
20. Warakija	55
21. Waku jumpurujumpuru	57
22. Yalurrpalurrpungulu	59
23. Yarlangki	61
24. Yinirnti	63
25. Warnamarra	65

26. Jurdurrungkarni	67
27. Jipily jipily	69
28. Wulpayi	71
29. Kurlarda wangardijarrili	73
30. Wawirrina	75
31. Wurnapa ngarrkanta	77
32. Ngati mulyumulyu	79
33. Ngapakurla	81
34. Lyinjirrmarlinja	83
35. Wardijayi	85
36. Junpurla	87
37. Yirarri-rarri-manu	89
38. Pinapi-rnalu	91
Plates	92
References	94
Appendix 1: Correspondences between verses in the Yuupurnju and *Karntakarnta* song cycles	96
Appendix 2: Sequence of verses on the recordings	98

List of figures

Figure 1. Warlpiri subsection (or skin group) system. 3
Figure 2. Significant places related to the Yuupurnju song cycle. 8
Figure 3. A guide to the information presented in this book. 14

Preface

Song cycles are foundational to the ceremonies in which Warlpiri people celebrate the ancestral beings that created their world and in which they draw on ancestral power to affect people's lives today. The ancestral beings emerged from the subterranean spirit world and through their activities fashioned the many features of the landscape, including creating sacred places. Especially sacred are places where the ancestral beings emerged from and returned to the ancestral world. In the many different song cycles, the travels and actions of particular ancestral beings are traced as they moved from place to place. The ancestral beings, their travels, the places they created, and the laws and customs they laid down for people are all known as part of the *Jukurrpa*, the Dreaming as it is called in English.

In this book, we document one important song cycle, Yuupurnju, associated with the Warlpiri male maturity ceremony that transforms boys into men. The songs trace the travels of a group of ancestral women taking boys to a ceremony far away from where they set out at Minamina, in the west of Warlpiri country.

Recording this song cycle was the idea of Warlpiri Elder Henry Cooke Anderson Jakamarra from Lajamanu community in the Northern Territory. He was concerned about the future of the Yuupurnju song cycle, and felt it was important to have it recorded for the benefit of future generations. While songs Henry Cooke Jakamarra recorded here are still sung at some Warlpiri male maturity ceremonies, another Warlpiri song cycle about a related group of women is now more commonly sung.

Henry Cooke Jakamarra singing Yuupurnju, Lajamanu, NT.
Image from recordings of the song cycle, 2013.

The book includes the words of the songs, interpretation in English as given by Jakamarra and Warlpiri Elders Jerry Patrick Jangala OAM, Wanta Steven Patrick Pawu-Kurlpurlurnu Jampijinpa and Steven Dixon Japanangka, and the verses (text and rhythm) by musicologist Myfany Turpin. Forewords by senior custodians Jerry Patrick Jangala and his son Wanta Jampijinpa provide a rationale for the book.

Forewords

Jerry Patrick Jangala OAM

Yuwayi nyampu, nyampu karna yirri-puraya Yuupurnju. Yuupurnju karna yirri-pura. Yuupurnju karna yirrarni warlalja yapaku, kuja-rnalu waja-waja-manulku. Ngula yirnalu ina yirrarni wayi yingarlu pinarra-jarrimi marda nyampu purdangirli-warnu or kulkurru-paja or kamparru-rla warlaljaku nyampuku Yuupurnjuku. Yangka kurdu-yunpu warlalja-kurlu yinga kurdu marda manyu-pinyi manu pinarri-mani Yuupurnju nyampu-kurlu. Warlpiri-kirlangu warlalja, Warlpiri-jarra-kurlangu, kurlarra-kurlangu, kurlarra karlarra-kurlangu, kakararra yatijarra-kurlangu.

Yes, this one, this one, I'm talking about Yuupurnju. Yuupurnju, I'm documenting it for our Warlpiri people, because we have lost it. This one we learn perhaps from people who went before us, adults can learn them, from those who came before us. It's for us Warlpiri people, this Yuupurnju. Maybe children can, with their families, maybe children perhaps celebrate with it, as their Elders are teaching them about this one. It belongs to Warlpiri families, it belongs to Warlpiri people in the south, it belongs to Warlpiri people in the south and west, it belongs to Warlpiri people in the east and north.

Nyampuju warlalja Yuupurnjuju. Manu wiri-nyayirni yali-rlipa nyurnu-nyurnu-rlangu pinarri-manu manulpa ngarrkakujurnu ngulakurlu-rlu-juku warlalja-kurlurlu.

This one, Yuupurnju, is for our families, and it is very important. Our ancestors who have passed away taught it to the next generations, the Elder men used to teach it to the men who were preparing for ceremonies in our families. It's for our Warlpiri families.

Warlalja Warlpiri-patuku nyampu Kanakurlangu-jangka Minamina-jangka Minamina-kurra manu nganayi-wiyi Kunajarrayi-wiyi-ngirli. Ngari karna ngajuju yirri-puraya kaji-kaji yatuju-ngurlu-rlu-jala kakararra-ngurlurlu ka kurlarni-kulkurru-jarra kularni-nyarra-warnu warlaljaji yapaji. Ngula marda yangka pinarri-jarri yingalpa marda purda-nyanjarla pinarri-jarriyalku yapa warlalja-marri ngulaku.

It travels from Kanakurlangu, from Minamina, to Minamina, and another one is from Kunajarrayi. I'm telling this from stories that I learned from our Elders. I'm from the north-east side. These songs are from the middle near the south side. All the Warlpiri people can learn this songline. If we listen to it, we can learn it. All the Warlpiri people can do this. We celebrate with this song series, children can learn it all because it is taught.

Yangka yinga manyu-karri marda kurdu-yunpu marda or nyiyarla marda nyiyaku marda yangkaju pinarri-maninjaku manu ngulakunya karna yirrarni. Nyampu Nungarrayirli kuja kangurnu wangkanja-kurlangu ngula karna yirrarni kaji-kaji kulkurrurni kulkurru-rla yapaku Warlpiri-patu-ku. Manu kakararra-kurla yali kuja kakararra-purda yapa nyinanjarrarni, Yanmatjirri Yalyawarri kapala nyinanja-yani nyanungu-kurlu palka-kurlu. Ngulanya karna yirrarni.

I'm putting all this together. Nungarrayi [Carmel O'Shannessy] is here with me listening and writing it down for everyone, for everyone in the middle age-groups. It is for Warlpiri people to the east, for everyone who is in the eastern area, where Anmatyerr and Alyawarr people have got these Dreamings too. This is what I'm putting together.

Kala nyampurlaju lawalku karnalu purlka-purlka-wangurlalku karnalu wapa-karra nyina kuja karli Jakamarrarlu japantarra-pinyi. Nyampu ah nyanungu Yuupurnju purlapa, ngula warlalja yalumpuju warlalja ngalipaku.

Nowadays we are losing some knowledge. Our Elders have gone, Jakamarra and I are the only senior ones here who have this knowledge about singing these traditional songs, this Yuupurnju song cycle and ceremony, for the Warlpiri people, for us, the Warlpiri people.

Ngula na karna nyampu yirri-puraya. Marda yunpa yangka junga-nyayirni pinarri-jarri manu university-rla-rlangu marda yingangkurlu ngula-rlangu-rla kajinkirli yirrarni marda marl-ngayi mardarni, yeh ngula nyuntuluku yapaku Warlpiri-patu-ku-wiyi, Warlpiri warlaljaku-wiyi. Nyuntu-nyangu kuruwarri nyampuju, nyuntu-nyangu-kurlu wankaru-kurlu. Nyuntu-nyangu-kurlu ngalijarra-kurlangu-ku-rla.

This is what I'm saying. Maybe you can learn it, at universities perhaps, when you do this you can maintain it. Yes, like that. It is for you, for Warlpiri people, for our families. It is your Dreaming, for you to keep it alive. It is yours, it is ours together.

Kala ngaju-warnu nyampu jintangkulku ngari yirrarni purlka-purlka-kuju. Lawalkurla karrija purlka-purlka-kuju warlaljakuju. Nyampuju karna yirrarni ngari kakararra-ngurlulku. Yangka pina-manjin-purranjarlu kujarna purda-nyangu manu kujarna yali-wana, yalumpurla-kula purlkarra-jarrija nyampurla-kula manyungkaji.

But this one from me now is for old people. Our old people are gone now. I'm from the east just putting this one here now, the one that I remembered, moving from there, putting it here, in fun.

Manyu-jala karna ngarrirni but manyu-wangu nyampuju junga manyu-wangu. Junga-nyayirni yapaku warlaljaku. Ngulajuku karna nyampunya yirri-puraya. Kajinpa ngampurrparlu pina-mani ngulaju ngulajuku. Ngulaji nyuntuluku nyampunya karnangku wangkami yapa-kuju ngulaju. Ngula karna wangka ngajuju yangka Jangala. Ngula karna wangka purlkalku. Nyampurna-nyarra yirri-puraja mardakangku warlalja. Ngulajuku.

I know I'm saying that it is fun, but it is really true, it is very important. This is what I'm saying. If you are really interested to be taught it, that's good, it's for you. This is what I'm saying to you, it is for Warlpiri people. I'm Jangala speaking as a Warlpiri Elder. This is what I've said to you, keep it for yourselves, for Warlpiri people. That's all.

Jerry Patrick Jangala OAM,
Lajamanu community,
13 December 2021.
Transcribed and translated by
Carmel O'Shannessy and Sabrina Granites Napangardi.

Wanta Steven Patrick Pawu-Kurlpurlurnu Jampijinpa

All these songs that old Henry Cooke Jakamarra sings, and that old Jerry Jangala sings, they are the songs of all the Warlpiri people, plus Yanmajirri (Anmatyerr) and Yalyawarri (Alyawarr) people. They all have the same songlines, even though they are different language groups. The songs bring back a lot of memories, a lot of memories. We should let the *walyajarra*, our ancestors, sleep on, but we should remember them. All the songs in this set are called Yuupurnju. People also call them *Kurdiji*, because they're part of a *Kurdiji* ceremony song series, *Marnakurrawarnu*. One section of *Kurdiji* is called *Marnakurrawarnu*. Jangala is saying that it's *manyu-kurra* "fun" or "celebration", but that it's also serious. We want to bring this song cycle back. If there's an opportunity to re-learn this one, I hope you do it well and study all these songlines. Even though it isn't a complete songline, it's enough to get you started, *yuwayi* "yes". So in the name of all the *walyajarra* "ancestors", yes, let's celebrate them, too, when we've learned these songs.

Wanta Steven Patrick Pawu-Kurlpurlurnu Jampijinpa,
Lajamanu community,
13 December 2021.

List of contributors

Henry Cooke Jakamarra. Image from the recordings of the song cycle, 2013.

Henry Cooke Anderson Jakamarra† was a senior Warlpiri man, who passed away in July 2022. He grew up in the pre-colonial Warlpiri style of living on the land, travelling through the country with his family and learning skills of survival and knowledge of songs and stories. He experienced the early period of contact between Warlpiri and non-Indigenous people and saw his traditional Country taken over by non-Indigenous people to mine its precious metals. He subsequently worked from the age of about 12 years at a wolfram mine at Luurnpakurlangu, on Mount Doreen station, Northern Territory, and for the police in different locations in the Northern Territory. He was a resident of Lajamanu community from soon after the community was established, and lived there with his family until he became a resident at Rocky Ridge Nursing Home in Katherine. Considered by other Warlpiri to be one of the most knowledgeable Elders, he took a leading role in ceremonial and traditional practices, and in teaching traditional skills and knowledge to younger generations, for many years. Jakamarra has in recent years been recognised by Australian law as the Traditional Owner of the Country on which the Granites mine is located. For more information about Jakamarra's life story, see the 2020 film *Kaja-warnu-jangka* "From the Bush", Pintupi Anmatyerr Warlpiri Media and Communications (PAW Media). Producers: Maxwell Walma Tasman Japanangka and Carmel O'Shannessy (available at https://bit.ly/4b2EKCE).

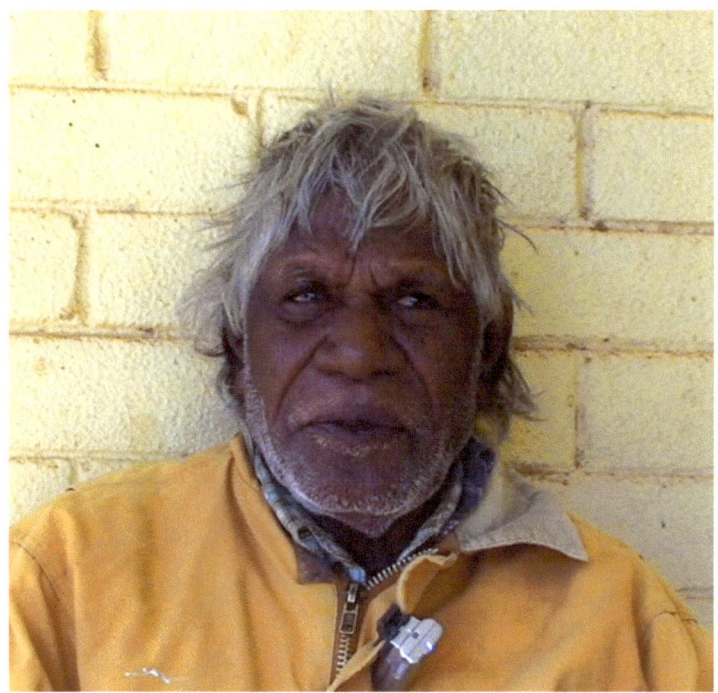

Jerry Patrick Jangala OAM © Carmel O'Shannessy 2008

Jerry Patrick Jangala OAM is a senior Warlpiri man now in his eighties, who also grew up in the traditional Warlpiri lifestyle, travelling the land and learning the songs, stories and bush skills from his family. He was one of the first group of people to be taken to the site of Lajamanu community in 1948–49, where he worked to build the infrastructure of the community, including roads, an airstrip, fences and buildings. He was also a drover and stockman on cattle stations, often far from Lajamanu. He later became a celebrated pastor in the Baptist Church. He is known across the Northern Territory and beyond for his skills, deep knowledge and teaching of both traditional Warlpiri language and culture and Christianity. Jangala is a key person in the cultural event called the Milpirri Festival, an evening of songs, stories and dance performed in Lajamanu every second year in collaboration with Tracks Dance Company. He lives in Lajamanu community with his family and continues to be a central figure of knowledge and authority for both Warlpiri and non-Warlpiri people. For more information about Jangala's life story, see *Kaja-warnu-jangka* "From the Bush", Pintupi Anmatyerr Warlpiri Media and Communications (PAW Media) 2020. Producers: Maxwell Walma Tasman Japanangka and Carmel O'Shannessy (available at https://bit.ly/4b2EKCE)).

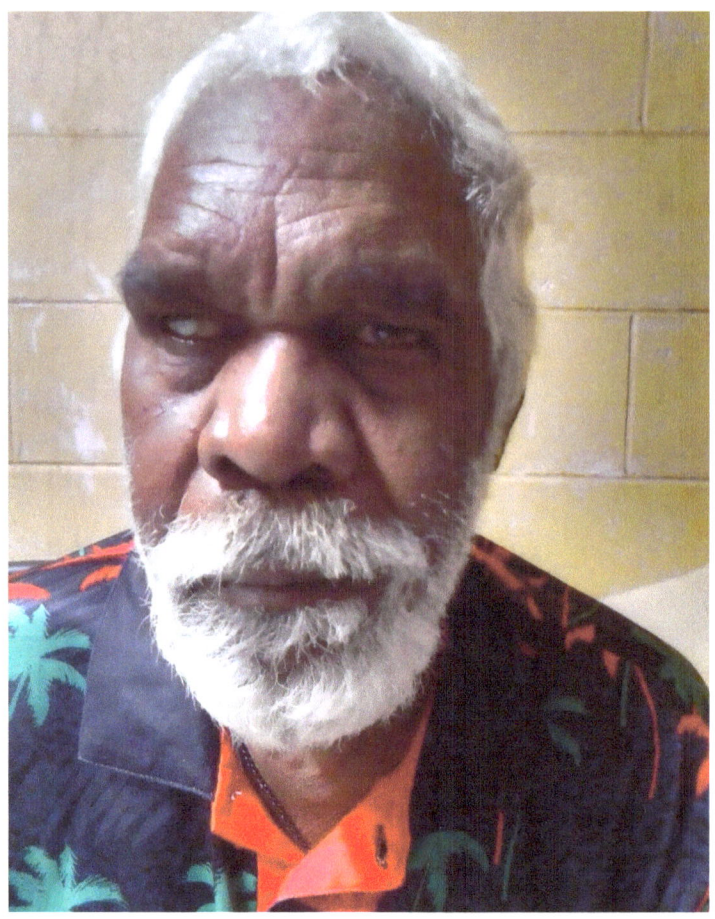

Steven Dixon Japanangka © Kimberley Dixon Napangardi 2022

Steven Dixon Japanangka† was a senior Warlpiri man living in Lajamanu community. Younger than Jakamarra and Jangala, he grew up in the 1960s, a time when the Warlpiri were stripped of their independence and lived under a government welfare regime. As an adult, he was active in continuing ceremonial practices. He was involved in community programs such as those to prevent family violence. He lived in Lajamanu community with his family, and passed away in 2023.

Wanta Steven Patrick Pawu-Kurlpurlurnu Jampijinpa
© Maxwell Walma Tasman Japanangka and PAW Media 2020

Wanta Steven Patrick Pawu-Kurlpurlurnu Jampijinpa is a senior Warlpiri man, and a son of Jerry Patrick Jangala. Jampijinpa grew up in Lajamanu community, learning from his father and other senior men and women about Warlpiri *Jukurrpa*, and learning to understand *kardiya* (non-Indigenous) culture and how the two can be reconciled. Jampijinpa is also a key person in the creation of the Milpirri Festival. He was an ARC Discovery Indigenous Award Fellow at the Australian National University School of Music, 2012–2015. He lives in Lajamanu community with his family.

Carmel O'Shannessy. Photo by David Spellman 2017.

Carmel O'Shannessy is a linguist and educator who was resident in Lajamanu community for four years (1998–2001), working to support the teaching and learning of Warlpiri and English in the bilingual education program in the school. Since 2002, she has visited the community at least annually for periods of weeks or months, documenting a newly-emerged mixed language, Light Warlpiri, child language development and multilingualism and traditional song cycles. She is an Associate Professor at the School of Literature, Languages and Linguistics, Australian National University.

Myfany Turpin 2018.

Myfany Turpin is a linguist and musicologist who has been working on Australian Aboriginal songs and languages since 1996. Her research interests include the relationship between language and music, especially of lesser-known cultures, and identifying ways to support the continuation of endangered languages and performance arts. More specifically, her work examines Aboriginal song-poetry and its relationship to spoken languages. She is also involved in linguistic documentation of the Aboriginal language Kaytetye, as well as Indigenous ecological knowledge and the lexicon in Arandic languages. She has collaborated on traditional Warlpiri women's song projects. She is an Associate Professor at the Sydney Conservatorium of Music.

Acknowledgements

We wish to thank the many people who contributed to this work, especially Yamurna Oldfield Napurrurla, Sabrina Granites, Tinyi Kimberley Dixon Napangardi, Central Land Council, Pintupi Anmatyerr Warlpiri Media and Communications (PAW Media), Warnayaka Art Centre, members of Lajamanu community, Fiona Walsh, Wendy Baarda, Grace Koch, Mary Laughren, David Nash, Nicolas Peterson, Georgia Curran, Jean Jia Jia Wong, photograph contributors and manuscript reviewers.

Funding for this project was provided by the University of Michigan, the Australian National University, the University of Sydney, Australian Research Council (ARC) Future Fellowship projects FT190100243 and FT140100783, and Newmont Tanami Pty Ltd.

Introduction to Warlpiri song cycles

Carmel O'Shannessy and Myfany Turpin

Traditional song cycles are part of foundational Warlpiri beliefs and practices known as *Jukurrpa,* Dreaming. The performance of a song cycle is part of ritual actions and events. The song cycles are sung by senior people in ceremonies. Some are only performed by women, such as *yawulyu* "public women's ceremonies" (Curran 2017), and there are some only sung by men, such as Yuupurnju, which women dance to. There are also others that only men can perform and listen to. Song cycles are sung in ceremonies for different purposes; for example, during male maturity rites, to resolve conflict or to make rain (Wild 1975). This book presents one song cycle, Yuupurnju, that forms part of a male maturity ceremony.

We first provide some contextual information about Warlpiri song cycles and Yuupurnju, the song cycle represented in this book. Each song in the cycle is then presented as a sung text and rhythm (verse), with the words on which the song is based, and their interpretation as given by the senior Warlpiri men.

The context of traditional Warlpiri songs

Two central aspects of Warlpiri life are key to understanding the context and importance of traditional songs. One is the Warlpiri belief system, *Jukurrpa*, translated into English as "Dreaming" or "Dreamtime" (e.g. Nicholls 2014), "everywhen" (Stanner 1979: 24), or "creation time" (Dobson 2007). The other is the system of social classification by subsection groups, known colloquially as the "skin" or "skin group" system, an abstract model of the named kinship relationships such as mother, father etc., relevant to all aspects of *Jukurrpa*, ceremonies and also everyday interactions. All traditional Warlpiri songs are linked to *Jukurrpa*. Senior Warlpiri woman Jeannie Nungarrayi Herbert† explains the everyday presence of *Jukurrpa* for Warlpiri people:

> The Jukurrpa is an all-embracing concept that provides rules for living, a moral code, as well as rules for interacting with the natural environment. The philosophy behind it is holistic – the Jukurrpa provides for a total, integrated way of life. It is important to understand that, for Warlpiri and other Aboriginal people living in remote Aboriginal settlements, The Dreaming isn't something that has been consigned to the past but is a lived daily reality. We, the Warlpiri people, believe in the Jukurrpa to this day. (Cited in Nicholls 2014)

The integration of kinship into *Jukurrpa* was explained by musicologist Stephen Wild:

> Patrilineal descent groups are the basic social groups in Walbiri[1] society. Each descent group is associated mystically with several sacred sites, which consist of notable features in the countryside: hills, rock formations, water holes, watercourses, stands of trees, fields of yams, caves, and the like. These sites are believed to have been created by supernatural beings in a timeless dimension of existence known in Australian English as the Dreamtime,[2] a concept common to all Australian Aboriginal peoples. The Dreamtime is spoken of as the remote past, but it also has a present existence in the form of its supernatural power which is responsible for the fertility of the country and of the Walbiri. As well as creating the features of the countryside and maintaining its fertility, the supernatural beings of the Dreamtime are believed to have instituted Walbiri culture; the validity of Walbiri patterns of social life is believed to have its source in the actions of the Dreamtime beings as commemorated in the religious rituals of the Walbiri. The adult members of a descent group, particularly the males, are responsible for performing the commemorative rites associated with the sacred sites on the descent group's estate. An estate is defined as the country in which are located the sacred sites having a mystical relationship with a descent group. It is not necessarily continuous. (Wild 1975: 6–7)

In the subsection (or skin) system, each individual has one of eight subsections, with distinctions by gender, making 16 names in all. Skin names of males begin with J, and skin names of females begin with N. In addition, there are a number of junior skin names for each subsection. An individual is born into the system according to the skin classifications of their parents. The system situates an individual's relationship with every other individual, including

---

1   Walbiri is an earlier spelling of Warlpiri, used by Wild (1975).
2   Wild (1975) used the term Dreamtime whereas in this book we use Dreaming.

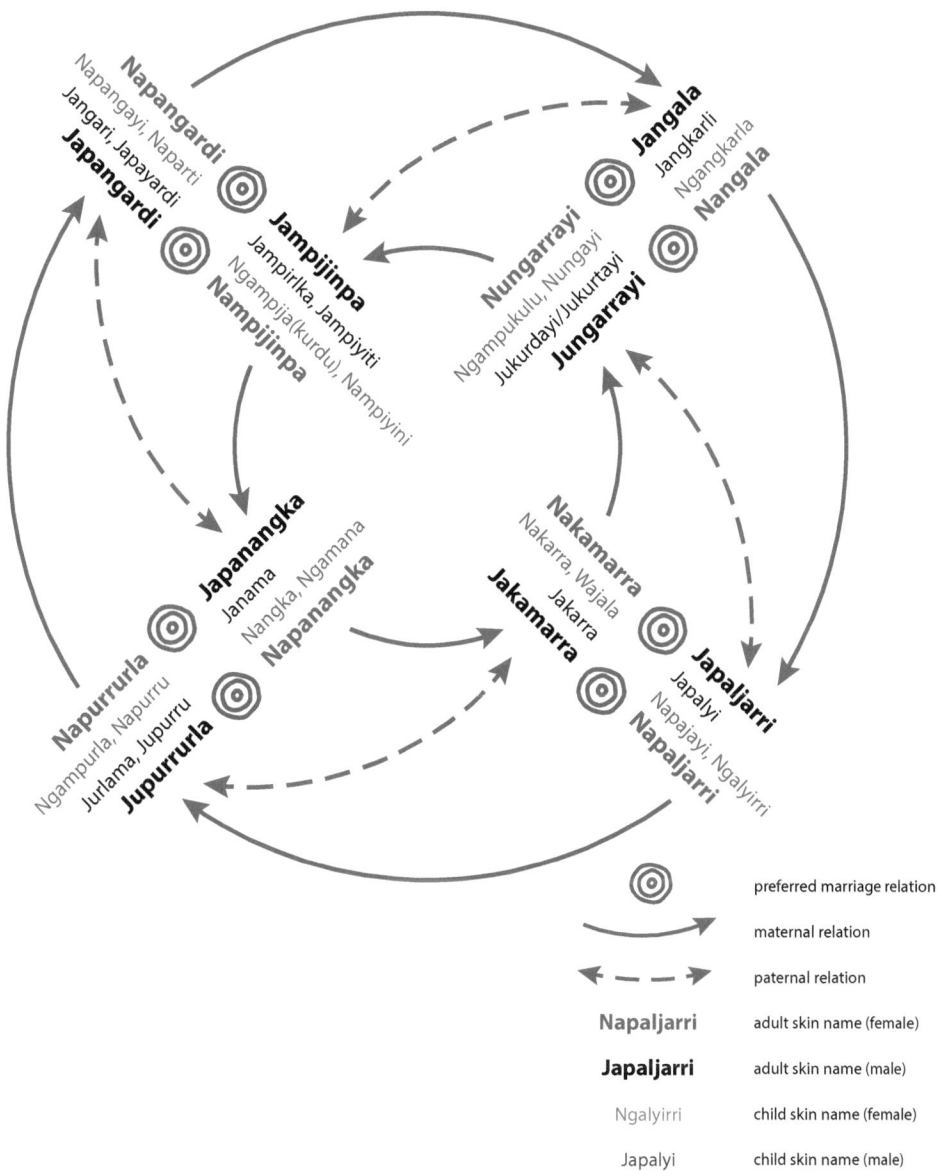

Figure 1. Warlpiri subsection (or skin group) system. From Laughren et al. (2022: 1361).

the skin category from which a spouse would come. The system is both biological and classificatory; for instance, a person refers to their biological mother, and women with the same subsection or skin name, as mother. A graphical representation of the system is provided in Figure 1.

Figure 1 shows the eight skin groups with a name for each gender, and the relationships between them. Each pair represents a brother and sister; for instance, *Jangala* and *Nangala* are brother and sister. The solid line arrow

( ) shows the relationship of mother to child, and the double-headed broken line arrow ( ) shows the relationship of father to child. The concentric circles show preferred spouse relationships. For example, *Jangala* and *Nangala* are the children of *Jampijinpa* (father) and *Napangardi* (mother). The preferred marriage partner of *Jangala* is *Nungarrayi*, and the preferred marriage partner of *Nangala* is *Jungarrayi*.

In everyday life in Warlpiri communities, subsection terms are the most common way of addressing people and referring to others. Although Warlpiri people have both Warlpiri and English-derived individual and family names, and use kin terms such as mother, older sister and so on, the subsection terms are the most commonly used terms.

Underlying the subsection system is a division of two patrimoieties between which the subsections are divided:

> Walbiri music and dance are performed in the context of magical and religious rites … Songs are arranged in long song cycles, and the text of each cycle refers to the activities of a Dreamtime being in his[3] travels across the country. Particular songs are associated with particular sacred sites along the traveling route of a Dreamtime being, so that one song cycle is associated with the estates of several patrilineal descent groups (Wild 1975: 9–10).

The sites are linked with different patrilineal descent groups, and the specific *Jukurrpa* stories and songs are the responsibility of those groups. Only a few of the twenty or so patrilineal groups of the *kirda* patrimoiety are the primary custodians of any song cycle and the *Jukurrpa* that it represents. Likewise, only a few of the twenty or so patrilineal descent groups that make up the opposite patrimoiety have the primary task of being *kurdungurlu* (managing custodians) of the *Jukurrpa* being celebrated. For all ceremonies, the participation of members of both patrimoieties is required. (Wild 1975: 39)

The performances of song cycles typically involve group singing during a ceremony, often led by one or a small number of senior singers who are *kurdungurlu*, collaborating with the traditional custodians or owners of the cycle. Percussion is provided by clapping two boomerangs together, or beating sticks (or more recently empty plastic bottles) on the ground. Typically, the song cycles recount aspects of the ancestral beings' travels across Warlpiri Country, as the ancestors themselves held ceremonies, sang and danced at specific sites. There are different genres, or types, of song cycles, and one of these is the type associated with the male maturity ceremony, called *kurdiji* (a word meaning

---

3   Ancestral beings may be either male or female.

"shield" (Laughren et al 2022: 418)). Other types of song cycles include *yilpinji* (love songs) (Wild 1975: 137; Curran 2010: 103), *Jardiwanpa* (conflict resolution ritual) (Wild 1975: 140; Gallagher et al. 2014) and *mikawurru* (rain-making rituals) (e.g. Wild 1975: 133). For details of different types of Warlpiri ceremonial songs, see Wild (1975), Curran (2010), Laughren et al. (2016) and Gallagher et al. (2014).

Male maturity ceremonies are held in Lajamanu community annually in the summer, or the wet season. The first day and night are referred to as the *Marnakurrawarnu* (written as *mana-kura-wanu* in Wild 1975: 284) and a second stage as the *Kirridikirdawarnu*. The whole ceremony may be called *kurdiji* because of the practice of displaying painted shields to the novices on the first night (Meggitt 1962: 284, cited in Wild 1975: 100). During the all-night ceremony, men, women and children gather at the ceremonial ground, the men singing the song cycle throughout the night and the women dancing. Curran (2020) provides observation and analysis of the role and importance of *kurdiji* ceremonies for Warlpiri people:

> *Kurdiji* ceremonies have remained an essential part of Warlpiri life while many other ceremonial forms have disappeared. Warlpiri people would argue that this is because these ceremonies are essential for "making young men": it is the only way for boys around the age of thirteen or fourteen, as well as their male and female family members (particularly their mothers and sisters), to be socialized into new roles, in which they have different responsibilities and are expected to behave in different ways. (Curran 2020: 123)

> In the *Kurdiji* ceremony, the emphasis is on being reborn into the world in a new role with a new social function, albeit after the symbolic death. It is held at night, a time associated with sleep and death, and thus the morning equates to reawakening and rebirth when the sun rises. The social status of the participants of the ceremony also ceases to be as it once was, as during the ceremony they neither hold the relationships they had prior to its start nor do they yet attain those that they will have at its conclusion. (Curran 2020: 127)

> Rituals such as *Kurdiji* are important because they maintain traditions that give meaning to people's lives in a rapidly changing world where traditional values are often hidden. The effectiveness of rituals in doing this derives precisely from their emergent nature, which gives the participants a great degree of control. Warlpiri people go to immense effort to hold ceremonies like *Kurdiji*, indicating the events' continuing importance to Warlpiri lives. (Curran 2020: 136)

Nicolas Peterson (personal communication 2022) also notes the importance of women in this ceremony:

> The focus of this male maturity rite is the relationship between males and females or men and women, which is why women are present for the greater part of the ceremony and absolutely vital to it. It would be meaningless without them. It is not just about turning boys into men but also about turning some women into mothers-in-law, sisters coming of age, and modifying the relationship of boys to their mothers.

Discussion of the complex interrelationships of Warlpiri ritual, kinship and gender is provided in Dussart (2000: 210), who concludes that the status and power of women are "irrefutably crucial to the reproduction of the *Jukurrpa* and correlative psychic health that accompanies that act of reproduction".

O'Shannessy has attended the public components of several ceremonies in the time that she has been in Lajamanu community. Families discussed with each other ahead of time who would be involved in the ceremony. In the days before a planned ceremony, a group of boys would be "caught", or physically located, and led by law men with specific roles in the ceremony to the ceremonial preparation area. High-pitched cries would be heard – a signal to others not to observe. If anyone noticed a group of men walking through the community at that time with a sense of purpose, they would duck their heads and hide because the event cannot be observed by others.

When the ceremonies take place, there is great excitement in the community. The ceremonies contain some restricted sections, which only men may participate in, but much of it is public. Within the public components, women occasionally need to bow their heads and close their eyes or cover themselves and their children with a blanket.

In preparation for the all-night part of the ceremony, men and women will have spent hours painting traditional designs on their bodies that are appropriate for the ceremony being performed. During this process, the women will have been singing *yawulyu* (traditional women's songs). Appropriateness includes the relationship of each person to the *Jukurrpa* and the subsections of the boys undergoing the ceremony.

People arrive at the ceremonial ground with food and bedding, usually "swags" – canvas covers with a thin foam mattress inside. The ceremony is held in the hot season in January–February, so the nights are fairly warm and minimal bedding is needed.

All ages are involved, from young children to Elders. Men sit facing east, with a small fire burning, and sing the songs with percussion, often beating sticks or empty bottles on the ground. The women form lines behind the men to dance. The dance movements differ according to the part of the song cycle being sung. The women alternate dancing with resting and sometimes napping. Children play, join the dancing, and sleep. For details of ceremonies, see Meggitt (1962), Wild (1975) and Curran (2010, 2020).

The Yuupurnju song cycle

Yuupurnju is a song cycle situated within the *kurdiji* ceremony. The song cycle relates to a traditional women's *Jukurrpa* story. A group of ancestral women travel across the country, dancing and singing at significant locations. The story and route of travel begins at Kanakurlangu and travels east to the Napperby Creek area and stops there (see Figure 2). The place name Kanakurlangu literally means "having a digging stick", and a digging stick is a symbol of women. In the song cycle, the women travel from west to east digging for *yarla* "yams". The people in the story went to Kanakurlangu and then separated into groups. Some went to Yinirnti-warrku warrku, the Lake Mackay area, a large salt lake near the Western Australia–Northern Territory border (Laughren et al. 2022: A1), while others went to Minamina. The Lake Mackay group became Nungarrayi and Napaljarri subsections, and it is the travels of this ancestral group of women that are more commonly followed at Yuendumu community. The Minamina group became Napangardi and Napanangka subsections. The men went back north and the women continued travelling east, and this is the ancestral route followed in the song cycle represented here. They travel through Janyinki and all join up at Pikilyi. Many of the verses tell where and how the women were dancing. Henry Cooke Anderson Jakamarra, the singer, describes the song cycle as women's Dreaming, and names himself as the person in a *kurdungurlu* relationship who can sing the songs. This was confirmed by other senior *kurdungurlu* and by a senior man in a *kirda*, owning patrimoiety, relationship to the song cycle.

For this song cycle, the *kirda*, or owning patrimoiety, are the people in the following subsection groups:

Nungarrayi/Jungarrayi   *Napanangka/Japanangka*
Napaljarri/Japaljarri   *Napangardi/Japangardi*

The *kurdungurlu*, or the patrimoiety of the managing custodians, belong to the following subsections:

Jangala/Nangala   *Jupurrurla/Napurrurla*
Jampijinpa/Nampijinpa   *Jakamarra/Nakamarra*

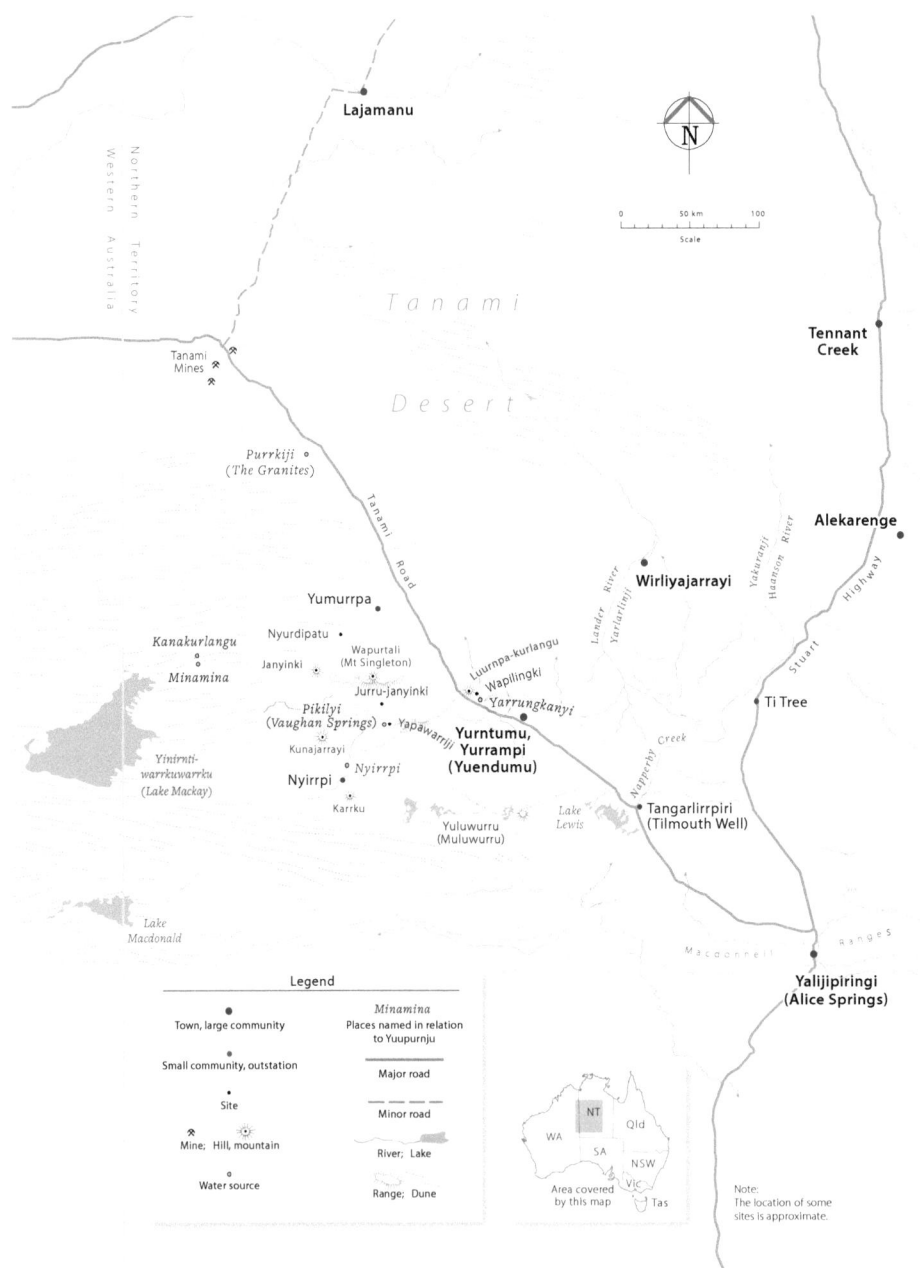

Figure 2. Significant places related to the Yuupurnju song cycle. Places named in the songs or commentaries are shaded. © Brenda Thornley 2022.

Yuupurnju as sung by Henry Cooke Anderson Jakamarra in 2013

Henry Cooke Anderson Jakamarra, a senior Warlpiri man and the singer of this song cycle, requested that these songs be recorded, kept safely and made available for future generations to learn from. Yuupurnju is normally sung only by a group of men during a man-making ceremony, from about 10pm until dawn. But Jakamarra was particularly interested in the song cycle being recorded and saved for younger men to learn, and so invited Carmel O'Shannessy to record him singing them solo. A selection of recordings can be viewed via the QR code above.

The recordings took place in August 2013 in the front yard of the house in which O'Shannessy was temporarily staying, across from where Jakamarra lived. He sang them in the daytime, singing for one to three hours most days, over three weeks, recorded by O'Shannessy. Over subsequent years, O'Shannessy worked with Jakamarra, Jerry Patrick Jangala OAM, Steven Dixon Japanangka and Wanta Jampijinpa to transcribe the words and provide interpretations of the meanings of the verses. Myfany Turpin transcribed the songs, explained their structure and produced Appendix 2.

The words of ceremonial songs are sometimes different from the words in everyday Warlpiri speech. Some of the words might have been used long ago and have changed over time. Other words are used only in traditional songs and not in everyday spoken Warlpiri; many of these resemble the everyday spoken words in neighbouring languages such as Anmatyerr and Kaytetye. Sometimes words are shortened or extended to fit a preferred rhythm. There can also be words that are the same as spoken language but that have complex meanings in the ceremonial context in addition to their everyday meanings. For these reasons, there is not always a one-to-one relationship between words in song and words in modern spoken Warlpiri. This is why interpretations from knowledgeable senior custodians are needed. Sometimes a verse, such as in Song 34 in this cycle, is in another language – in this case Anmatyerr, the language on the south-east of Warlpiri. This is because the ancestral dancers were at that point in a location that Anmatyerr people belong to.

Some of the songs in the Yuupurnju song cycle presented here were also sung in the *kurdiji* song cycle sung in Yuendumu in 2010, documented in Curran (2020). Different versions of a song cycle are sung in different communities. A song cycle may also change over time; that is, some songs are left out and other songs added to the song cycle, depending on by whom and where it is being performed. New songs can be introduced into a song cycle, and a whole new song cycle can be introduced to a community.

Musical structure of the song cycle

In this recording of Yuupurnju, Jakamarra sang some 1,335 songs, comprising 38 unique verses. Each song lasted 30–60 seconds. The number of iterations of each song varies – one was sung only once; most were sung many times, at different points in the whole cycle. A song consists of a short verse set to a particular rhythm that repeats until the end of the longer melody (see Wild 1984: 191–4; Turpin 2007). Depending on its length, the verse might be repeated four to six times until the song gradually fades out. After this, there is usually a break of a few seconds during which the singer might cough or take a sip of water and then begin the same verse again, sometimes starting and ending at a different place in the verse, changing the way the verse and melody interlock. Thus, these singings of the same verse are rarely identical. In between the change of verse, there is usually a longer break of up to two minutes. A list of the verses that were sung over the course of the recordings on which this book is based appears in Appendix 2.

There is no set pitch for each syllable of the verse because, as the text repeats, the syllables fall on different parts of the melody. Only the verses (rhythmic texts) of each song are written down in this book. We do not represent the melodic setting of each verse, as there are many ways a singer can align the verse and melody of a song and we do not wish to imply that each song always aligns in this way.

Most verses have two lines that repeat in an AABB pattern, although some verses have only one line. Often the lines within a verse are different lengths; and some lines occur in more than one verse. What is written in this book are actually verses: you can listen to the songs by scanning the QR code, while reading the verses. The verses are presented here according to the order in which they were first sung in this performance. In its ceremonial context, each verse is repeated many times during the night. Jakamarra frequently returned to a previously-sung verse later. For example, Jakamarra returned to Song 1 eight times throughout the performance. Appendix 2 lists each of the 1,335 songs that Jakamarra sang and identifies their verse number (Song 1, Song 2, etc.). The full recording (over 12 hours) can be accessed at the Australian Institute for Aboriginal and Torres Strait Islander Studies (AIATSIS).

How to use this book

All of the interpretations of verse meanings given here are publicly available. We do not try to interpret each verse on a word-by-word basis, but try to give a sense of the meanings of the verses. The verses are like poetry, and we hope that readers gain a sense of the poetry and imagery involved. Sometimes an interpretation of a verse wasn't given.

On each page, the words of the verse in Warlpiri are written near the top. Interpretations as given by Jerry Patrick Jangala and Steven Dixon Japanangka follow. QR codes are in the top right corner of the page and link to audio of the songs. The verse (the text and rhythm of the sung syllables) is set below the interpretations.

Wanta Jampijinpa explained that to learn the songs, the men usually learn five verses at one time, then learn another five, adding verses in groups of five.

There is a companion video hosted by PAW Media, showing Jakamarra singing two iterations of each verse, with the song words and very brief interpretations written. These are excerpts from the recordings made in 2013 on which this book is based, and can be watched at https://vimeo.com/916153442.

How songs are presented

A song consists of a verse – a rhythmic text – that repeats to a much longer melody. This book presents the verse (its words and rhythm), its interpretation as given by the senior Warlpiri men, and the meanings of words and phrases. It is important to listen to the accompanying audio to hear the melody and vocal timbre. Note that the speed of the songs may be faster than they are in performance, where there are multiple singers and dancers that the singers accommodate to. You'll also hear Jakamarra giving some interpretation and at times laughing.

Number and title

Each of the 38 songs is headed with a number and brief portion of song text as its name. Songs do not have official names and the order of songs can depend on the context in which they are performed. We use numbers and titles for ease of reference and aligning the accompanying audio.

Illustrations

For some verses, there are illustrations of women dancing. These are based on images of another public ceremony and are not intended to accurately reflect the designs that women would have on their bodies during a performance of the ceremony that belongs to the Yuupurnju song cycle. Rather, the images are intended to give a sense of the types of designs women wear, and of some of the movements depicted in the verses.

Verse

The text of each verse is presented next. Most verses consist of two lines, although six have only one line (Songs 13, 15, 16, 25, 26 and 35). In most verses with two lines, each line is repeated before moving on to the other line (a quatrain of AABB structure).

In some verses, it is only one line that repeats (a tercet of ABB). A repeating line is written twice, and the verses are written using Warlpiri spelling conventions (cf. Laughren et al. 2022). For example, below is the verse for Song 12, it consists of four lines:

> *Walangka juuturinyina*
> *Walangka juuturinyinayi*
> *Yarrpurnturla juuturinyinayi*
> *Yarrpurnturla juuturinyina*

Verses sometimes have sound patterning where the final vowel of the repeated line changes. For example, Song 12 is sung with different final vowels, underlined above. For a discussion of this sound patterning see Turpin 2021.

Musical figure

Following the words in the verse is a musical figure that shows the rhythm of the verse. The speed or tempo of the song is shown at the top of the musical figure. Underneath this is the rhythm of the vocal line(s). This begins with a time signature, which holds for both lines unless written for each line. Note that in some cases the time signature equals the number of beats per line, in which case no bar lines are shown. As a song is a repeating verse, the rhythm may differ slightly as it repeats, so the rhythm here is a broad representation. In some verses there is a tap beat, which is represented as a row of x's. The audio accessible via the QR code does not always include the tap beat, however other instances of each song are listed in Appendix 2, many of which include a tap beat. Underneath each rhythmic note is a single syllable. We have broken words up into syllables, to make it easy to see which syllable goes with which rhythmic note. Each line is divided into syllables, aligned with its rhythmic value. If a syllable is not sung, but it is in the verse, it is in brackets. Syllables that end in the sound represented in Warlpiri spelling as *ayi* (pronounced like the end of the English word "day") are written as *ay*, because they are sung as one syllable, never two.

English interpretation

After the verse, a brief interpretation follows in English, from the explanations given by Jakamarra and the other senior men.

List of words or phrases

Below the brief interpretation is a list of words or phrases in the verse followed by a colon, then an interpretation or explanation given by the senior Warlpiri men. Songs often use words and pronunciations not in contemporary spoken Warlpiri. So the word written in the interpretation is sometimes different to the word heard in the song. In addition, information is given about words from everyday spoken Warlpiri, where the authors feel confident about their form and meaning, or from the *Warlpiri Encyclopaedic Dictionary* (Laughren et al. 2022). Where we have drawn information from the dictionary, we refer to it as "*Warlpiri Encyclopaedic Dictionary*".

As explained earlier, we have not presented the songs with a word-for-word translation because the language of songs is very different to spoken Warlpiri. Sometimes the songs have very old words, or words from another language, or special forms only ever heard in song. Some word endings are less commonly heard in everyday speech but are common in traditional songs and narratives, such as the verb ending *-nya* (Song 4 *wangka-nya* "talking, producing sound", Song 33 *nguna-nya* "lying"), called the presentative form, which actualises "the situation in the narrative or performative present" (Laughren et al. 2022: 1334). Even when a word is also from spoken Warlpiri, the word may have many different additional meanings because songs use metaphors and other sorts of figurative language, and they can gain new meanings when performed in different contexts.

Some songs with the same or similar words also occur in a similar song cycle performed in Yuendumu in 2007, taking a more southern route (Curran 2020). The correspondences are indicated on each page as they occur, and are given in Appendix 1. The exact words and meanings given might differ between song cycles; for example, *wangkanya* "talk" versus *wangkaja* "talked".

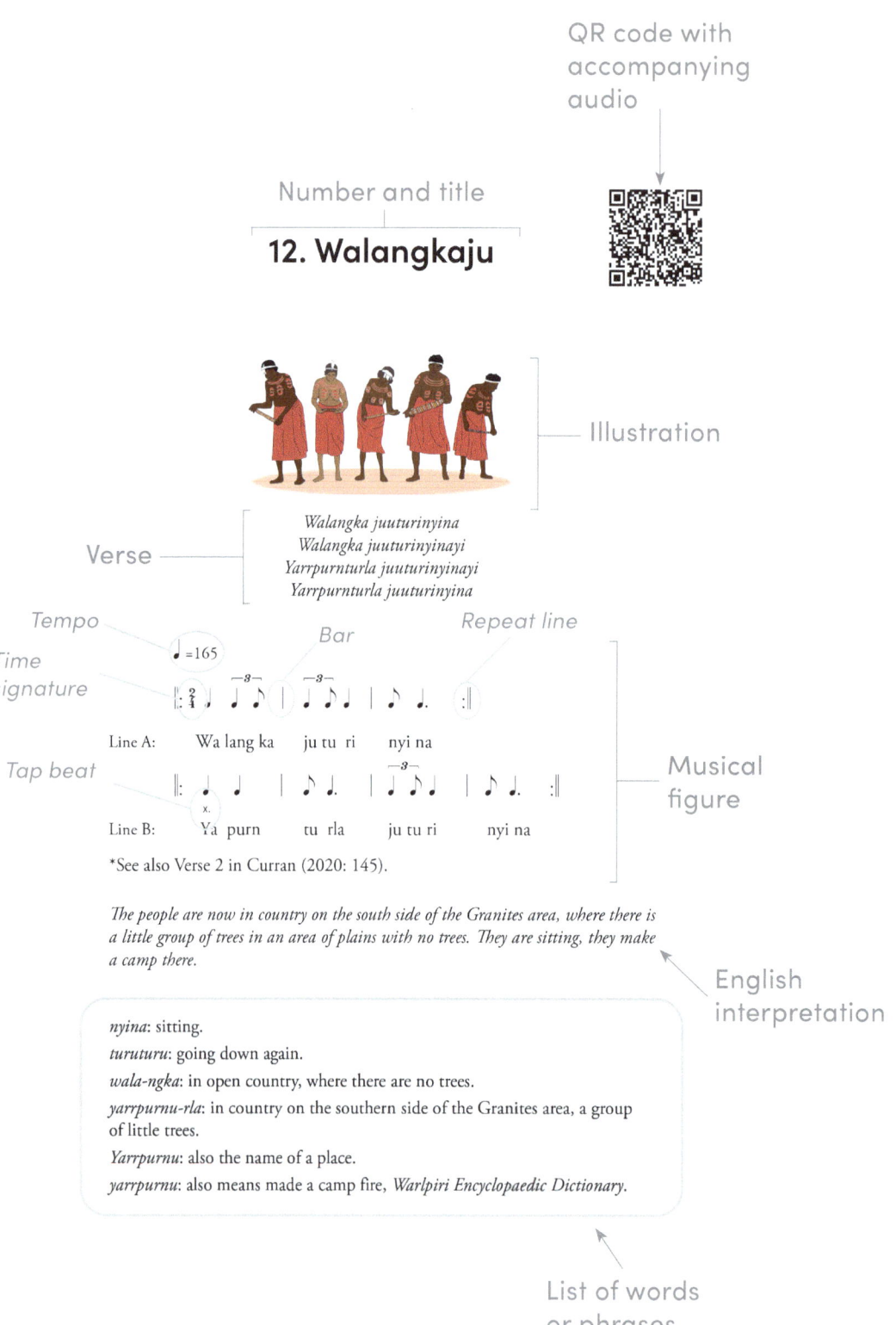

Figure 3. A guide to the information presented in this book.

List of musical conventions

‖   **Line** boundary. Most verses consist of two lines (A and B) which can be sung in either order.

‖: … :‖   **Repeat** line before commencing the other line. In most verses with two lines, each line is repeated before moving on to the other line.

| **Bar** boundary. Most lines consist of bars of an equal number of beats. Four verses have lines of an uneven number of beats and so are not divided into bars (Songs 2, 8, 9 and 27).

$\frac{3}{8}$ **Time signature**. Number of beats per bar, or per line if there are no bars (Songs 2, 8, 9 and 27). For most songs, the time signature holds for both lines (except Songs 8 and 20).

♩=150   **Tempo**. The number of beats per minute. Beats are expressed as a quarter ♩, half 𝅗𝅥 or eighth note ♪. For some songs, the tempo is given in number of clap beats x per minute.

x   **Tap beat** accompaniment. These are regular (isochronous) beats and so the duration of beats is not shown. Beating duration can be deduced from the tempo and time signature. In songs where the vocal part and percussive accompaniment divide the bar or line into a different number of beats (i.e. polyrhythm), this is indicated in the percussion accompaniment with a dot following the beat. Typically, the 3:2 cross-rhythm has the voice as triple and the accompaniment as duple, e.g.

♩♩♩ (3)   Hemiola. Three notes sung in the time of two.

♩♩♩♩♩ (5)   Five notes sung in the time of four.

♩♩ (2)   Two notes sung in the time of three.

𝄐   Fermata. This note/syllable is often prolonged.

Wulpararri or *yuwarra* "Milky Way," the path in the sky, rises over dunes.
© Harry Moore 2023

1. Kanaku kanakurla

Kanaku kanakurla yuwarra jarnti manu
Kanaku kanakurla yuwarra jarnti manu
Kanaku kanakurla yuwirripirnti manu
Kanaku kanakurla yuwirripirnti manu

♩ = 120

Line A: Ka na ku ka na ku rla   yu wa rra jarn ti ma nu
Line B: Ka na ku ka na ku rla   yu wi rri pirn ti ma nu

*This song has a fairly free rhythm, with the long notes in particular (such as ♩) sometimes lengthened.

A man called Yuwirripirnti, a Japangardi, picks up a digging stick and is moving it in his hand, looking at it. A person with the kinship (skin) name Japangardi is named Yuwirripirnti in the Jukurrpa.

---

jarnti: walking.
kana, yuwirri: digging stick.
Kanakurlangu: the name of a place, from where the song cycle begins.
manu: commonly occurs at the end of lines in songs; it can mean do, make, create.
pirnti: on the side.
yuwarra: also road and the road in the sky, the Milky Way, *wulpararri*.
Yuwirripirnti: the name of a person in the *Jukurrpa*.

Woman straightens the tip of a digging stick.
Photo by Areyonga School 2023 © Ara Iritija archive number AI-0290069-001

2. Karrinjapardi

Karrinjapardi karrinjapardi yakanarra
Karrinjapardi karrinjapardi yakanarra
Yuljurrurnpuju yuljurrurnpuju yakanarra
Yuljurrurnpuju yuljurrurnpuju yakanarra

♩ =77 beats per minute

Line A: Ka rri nja   pa rday   ka rri nja   pa rday   ya ka na na ka
Line B: Yul ju rum pul ju   Yul ju rum pul ju   ya ka na na ka

*This song has a fairly free rhythm.

The women are dancing. The sticks are on the ground beside the dancers, who are sitting. The women get up, pick up the sticks and dance, holding them in a digging motion, dragging the sticks across the ground.

---

karrinja-pardi: get up; "I want to get up, get the digging stick, and walk."
puju: "Quick!"
yakanarra: get up.

Lander River, Willowra, NT.
© Carmel O'Shannessy 2023

3. Tangkirrina

Yirla tangkirrina tangkirrina
Wurangkurlu ngarrka ngarrkanjarna

Line A: Yi rla tang   ki rri na   tang ki   rri na
Line B: U rang ku   rlu ngarr ka   ngarr ka   nja rnay

*The sequence of short notes, ♪♪♪, is sometimes sung with a longer last note, ♫♩.

The song is coming from the west to the east, from the south-west of Warlpiri Country.

yirangkurlu: this is an important ceremony. "We're going to dance for a long time, all night."

yulu-tankari-nga: the women are dancing now to the singing, with the digging sticks, and using their hands too, with no sticks.

ngarrka-ngarrka-jurnu: may mean that a boy is being brought into the male maturity ceremony now.

Kakalyalya, Major Mitchell's cockatoos at Yuendumu.
© Bob Gosford 2007

4. Wujuju-wangkanya

Wujuju-wangkanya wujuju-wangkanya
Yati ngangkamarda

Wu ju ju wang ka nya   wu ju ju wang ka nya ya ti ngang kay ma rda

*This song has a fairly free rhythm, with the long notes in particular sometimes lengthened. See also Verse 18 in Curran (2020: 154).

They are dancing at Wapilingki. The cockatoos are whispering, the women are looking and can't hear them because they are whispering. The people are calling the name of the cockatoo, who belongs to Pikilyi, or Vaughan Springs.

---

ngangkamarda: also called *kakalyalya*, is the Major Mitchell's cockatoo (*Lophochroa leadbeateri*).
wujuju-wangkanya: whispering. (Also pronounced *wijiji-wangkanya*.)
yajankurlarri: open.
yarti-ngangkamarda: all the birds are sitting around, the cockatoo is talking.
yati: "Oh, that's good!"

Red kangaroo in mulga habitat.
© Jenny Smits 2009

5. Yajankurlarri

Yajankurlarri
Yajankurlarri
Mulyurna wilpiri

Line A: Ya jan ku rla rray

Line B: Mu lyu rna wil pi ri

*See also Verse 16 Curran (2020: 153).

The people are looking at the two kangaroos, one kangaroo with an open nose, with a little mark between the nose and the mouth.

-rna: "I", first-person singular pronoun.
mulyu: nose.
wilpiri: hole (note *Kaytetye ilpere* "hollow"), wide nostrils.
yajankurlarri: open.

Acacia dictyophleba seeds in a desert bloodwood dish before being ground with water.
© Fiona Walsh 2015

6. Yanganpa

Yanganpala yanganpa
Yanganpala yanganpa
Yanganpala yijilyirrpunga
Yanganpala yijilyirrpunga

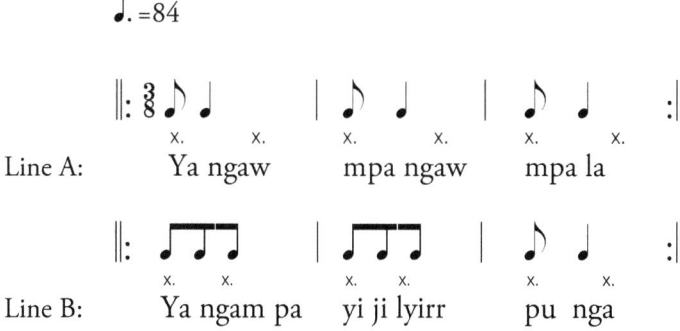

The women have got food now, seeds, ngurlu, they're grinding the seeds in a wooden dish. The women are going towards the north side, at Yapawarriji and at Pikilyi.

-npala: you two (dual subject), as in two people doing the action of grinding.
pungu: a grinding motion, grinding over and over. The seeds are from Pikilyi.
yanga: seeds, and grinding seeds.
yijilyirr-punga: a song word meaning grinding, related to the spoken word *yijirl-pinyi*, "grinding", *Warlpiri Encyclopaedic Dictionary*.

Rain clouds in the night sky, Lajamanu, NT.
© Carmel O'Shannessy 2016

7. Yarrintilarnu

Yarrintilarnu yananyawampa
Yarrintilarnu yananyawampa
Ngarlkajangarrkawu yananyawampa
Ngarlkajangarrkawu yananyawampa

The women dance flicking their fingers, to open up the light in the night sky, which is the initiate's birth right, he has to embrace that. Sparks fly from the women's fingers.

*The meanings of the individual words in this song were not given.

Ngalyarrpa "sandhill".
© Nic Gambold

8. Jinapi

Jinapi jinapi jinapi jinapi
Jitururrururru

Line A: Ji na pi ji na pi jay na pi ji na pi

Line B: Ji tu ru rru ru rru

It looks like sandhill country, they're sliding along.

jinapi jinapi: feet, referring to the feet of the women.

yutururrururru: slipping off the edge of something. The women's feet would slip down, slide down in the sand.

yujururrururru: sliding, slithering, *Warlpiri Encyclopaedic Dictionary*.

Miinypa "native fuchsia" grow in the hard mulga country.
© Myfany Turpin 2017

9. Miyinmarrirla

Miyinmarrirlayi yananyala
Miyinmarrirlayi yananyala
Yurnturlunturlu yananyala
Yurnturlunturlu yananyala

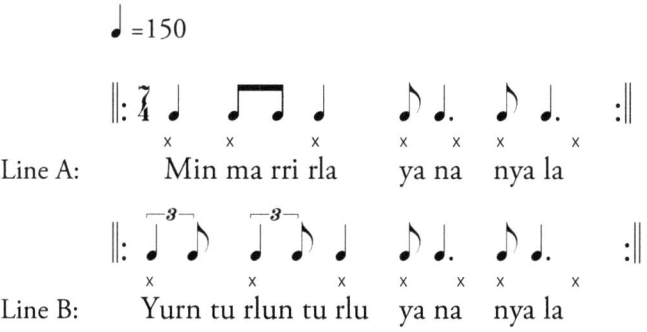

Line A: Min ma rri rla   ya na   nya la

Line B: Yurn tu rlun tu rlu   ya na   nya la

The women are walking through mulga country, with fuchsia bushes growing.

> *miyinmarrirla*: "We're in this tree country now."
> *miinypa*: native fuchsia (*Eremophila freelingii, Eremophila gilesii* subsp. *gilesii, Eremophila latrobei*), Warlpiri Encyclopaedic Dictionary.
> *yana*: going.
> *yananya*: a way to say "going", called the presentative form, common in traditional songs.
> *yananyala*: "We're going, we're walking on slightly different type of ground, a little bit hard, not sandy."
> *yurnturluturlu*: walking through the mulga country.

Manja "mulga" grows in hard ground, which is good for dancing on.
© Fiona Walsh

10. Manja kurrkurrku

Manja kurrkurrku wirntinya
Manja kurrkurrku wirntinya
Kanjarra kanjarra kurrkurrku wirntinya
Kanjarra kanjarra kurrkurrku wirntinya

The people are in an area with mulga trees. The women are dancing with their feet set wide apart. They continue dancing.

kanjarra: the same as *wantiki*, meaning legs wider open, spread out.

wirntinya: dancing; typically done by women. The ending *-nya* is common in *Jukurrpa* songs and stories.

kukulku: still doing.

manja: mulga (*Acacia aneura*); another word for it is *wardiji*. (See Song 35)

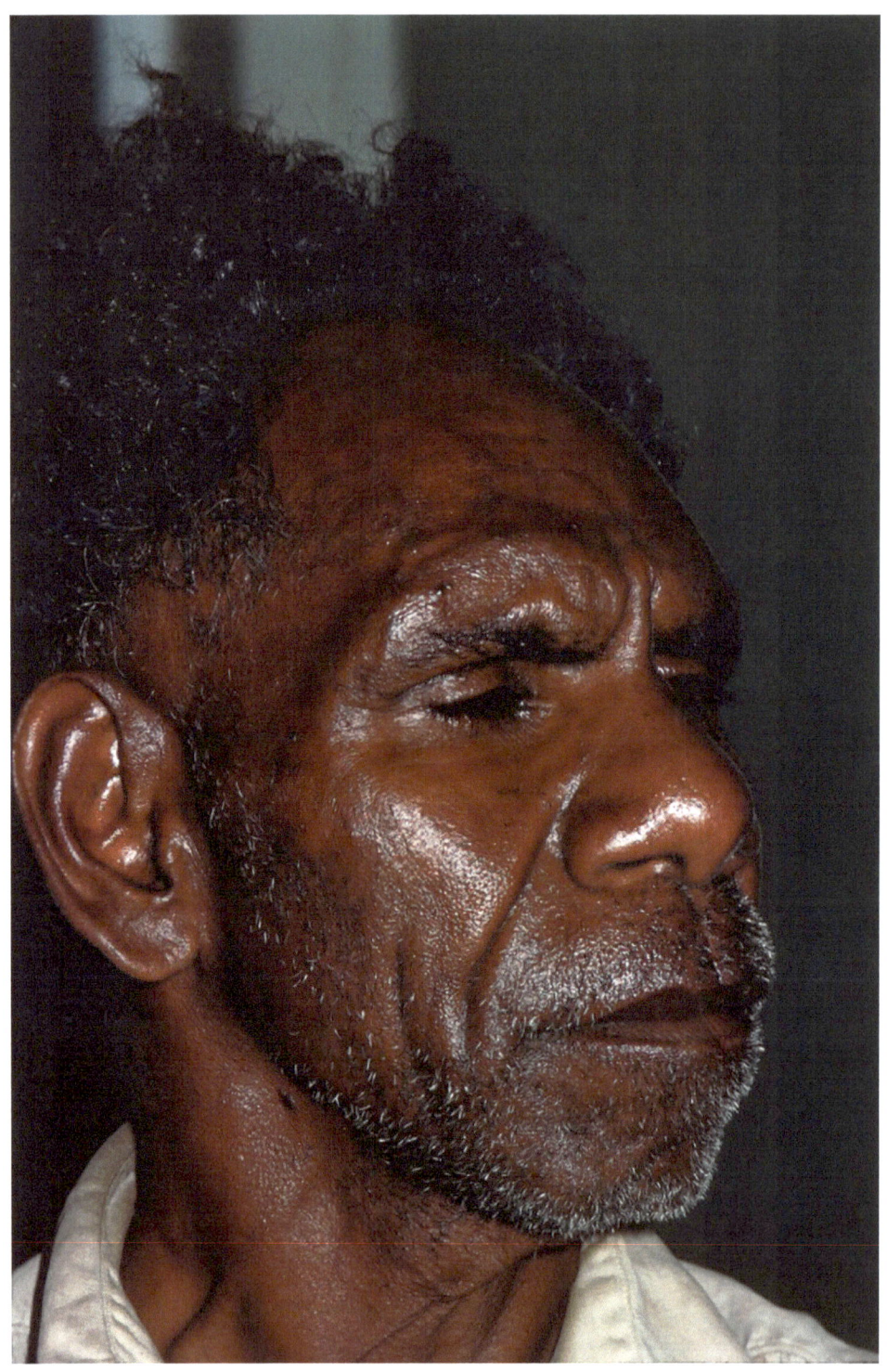

Henry Cooke Jakamarra, Lajamanu, NT.
© Ludo Kuipers 1976

11. Jujuju japarnti

nyartapa jujuju japarnti japarda parda palala wunayi

This song is incomplete. It was decided to keep the song in the documentation as part of the record of what Jakamarra sang.

Aerial view of a flat termite bed surrounded by spinifex and other grasses.
© Dave Wells 2023

12. Walangkaju

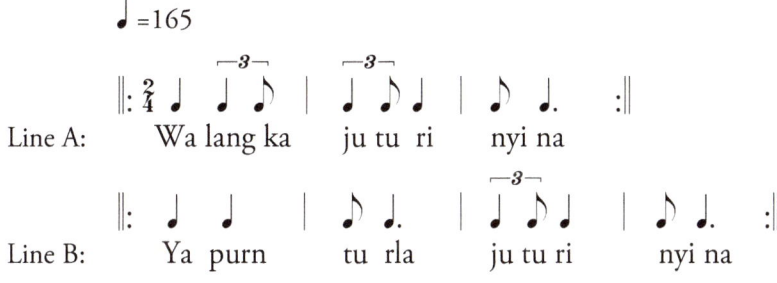

Walangka juuturinyina
Walangka juuturinyinayi
Yarrpurnturla juuturinyinayi
Yarrpurnturla juuturinyina

Line A: Wa lang ka   ju tu ri   nyi na

Line B: Ya purn   tu rla   ju tu ri   nyi na

*See also Verse 2 in Curran (2020: 145).

The people are now in country on the south side of the Granites area, where there is a little group of trees in an area of plains with no trees. They are sitting, they make a camp there.

---

nyina: sitting.

turuturu: going down again.

wala-ngka: in open country, where there are no trees.

yarrpurnu-rla: in country on the southern side of the Granites area, a group of little trees.

Yarrpurnu: also the name of a place.

yarrpurnu: also means made a camp fire, *Warlpiri Encyclopaedic Dictionary*.

Flat termite bed at Newhaven, NT.
© Fiona Walsh 2022

13. Palararrararra

Palararrararra parlanji yartampurr-karri yinjirinpunganya

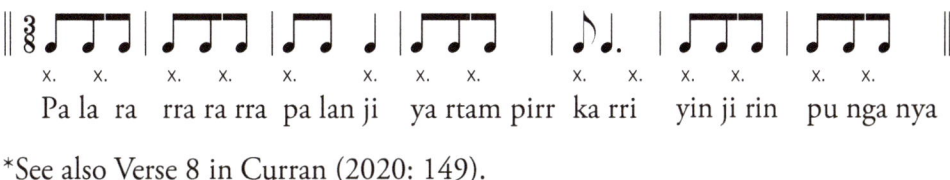

Pa la ra   rra ra rra   pa lan ji   ya rtam pirr   ka rri   yin ji rin   pu nga nya

*See also Verse 8 in Curran (2020: 149).

The women dance forward and back, in a place where there are flat termite beds and long, flat grass.

> *karri*: standing.
> *parlanji*: a really flat and clear place to dance, a good place to dance, on the flat termite beds.
> *yartanpurru karri*: a really flat and clear place to dance, good place to dance.
> *yatarnpirri*: absence of wind, calm, still, *Warlpiri Encyclopaedic Dictionary*.
> *yinjiri*: swamp grass (kangaroo grass), a type of long, flat grass which grows in that type of country and on the sides of creeks (*Themeda* spp., *Chrysopogon* spp.), *Warlpiri Encyclopaedic Dictionary*.

Henry Cooke Jakamarra singing Yuupurnju, Lajamanu, NT.
Image from recordings of the song cycle, 2013.

14. Kartiwirntinya

Kartiwirntinya kartiwirntinya
Kartiwirntinya kartiwirntinya
Kartimarangka kartimarangka
Kartimarangka kartimarangka

Line A: Ka rti wirn ti nya   Ka rti wirn ti nya
Line B: Ka rti ma rang ka   Ka rti ma rang ka

The women continue dancing. They hold their hands up a bit, at chest height, or clasp their fingers together behind their heads as they dance.

---

katu wirntinya: the women are holding their hands up a bit, chest height, or clasping fingers together behind their heads.

mara: hand. The Warlpiri word for this is *rdaka*. *Mara* is a Pintupi and Kukatja word.

wirntinya: women's dancing. A way to say "dancing", called the presentative form, common in traditional songs.

Two forms of stone axe with spinifex glue and handles.
© Christine Lennard 1989

15. Warrawarra

Warrawarra lajiwanpungu lajiwanpungu

Wa rra wa rra   la ji warn   pa ngu   la ji warn   pa ngu

*Jakamarra ends this song with a trilling sound. This is what the women sing at the end of each song.

The women are holding small axes, dancing.

> *pungu*: cutting.
> *rajiwanpungu*: easy to cut; dancing. When sung, it starts with an "l" sound.
> *warrawarra*: tomahawk or small stone axe (also *wala ngarrangarra*, an open place where they were dancing).

Aerial view of Lake Lewis, Anmatyerr country, NT.
© Peter Carroll

16. Yuluwurru

Yuluwurru lajiwanpungu lajiwanpungu

Yu lu wu rra la ji warn pa ngu la ji warn pa ngu

*See also Verse 48 Curran (2020: 169).

The women dance along the creek to Yuluwurru.

> *rajiwanpungu*: also in Song 15; here it probably refers to dancing. When sung, it starts with an "l" sound.
>
> *yuluwurru*: "salt lake"; also interpreted as getting tired from dancing. *Yuluwurru* or *Muluwurru* is also the name of the salt lake near Napperby Creek, on Anmatyerr Country. In Anmatyerr, it is called *Ilewerr*, Lake Lewis (Green 2008).

Minikiyi "native bees", *ngipiri* "eggs" and honey in a sugarbag hive.
© Myfany Turpin 2008

17. Yangipi yantakuyanta

Yangipi yantakuyanta yantakuyanta
Yangipi yantakuyanta yantakuyanta
Yangkipi kurlkudakurlku kurlkudakurlku
Yangkipi kurlkudakurlku kurlkudakurlku

♩=159

Line A: Ya ngi pi yan ta ku ya nta yan ta ku yan ta
Line B: Ya ngki pi kurl ku da kurl ku kurl ku da kurl ku

The women find little bees that make sweet honey.

> *kurlkudakurlku*: the bees inside the tree. It also means that the women's breasts are moving, representing the bees moving inside the tree.
>
> *ngipi*: the eggs from the baby bees that make wild honey. In spoken Warlpiri, *ngipiri* means egg of any sort.
>
> *yantakuyanta*: "We're going"; continuing to travel.

Parlintirri "women's fighting stick", which can also be used as a dancing stick.
© Myfany Turpin 2011

18. Karnta wurrparna

Karnta wurrpayi naparlirntirri
Yatiyi nganjalya ngajalya la

Line A: La karn ta wurr pay na pa rlirn ti rray

Line B: Ya ti ngan tha la ngan tha

*See also Verse 29 in Curran (2020: 160).

The women are holding their hands on the backs of their necks, bending down a little, looking down, as they dance all the way along.

> *karnta wurrpa*: the women are holding their hands on the back of their necks as they dance.
>
> *nganjalya ngajalya*: has the same meaning as *yatiyi* "Good!"
>
> *parlintirri*: they are using digging sticks, carrying them to protect themselves in the dance.
>
> *parlirntirri*: also interpreted as a fighting stick held out in front of a person to block a blow from an opponent's club, *Warlpiri Encyclopaedic Dictionary*.
>
> *yatiyi*: "That's good"; said when they protect themselves with a good swing with the digging stick. If you block the other stick, you could say, "*Yatiyi*!"

Henry Cooke Jakamarra singing Yuupurnju, Lajamanu, NT.
Image from recordings of the song cycle, 2013.

19. Waku mirntirrirla

Warlarrakuraka warlarrakuraka wirlpirla
Warlarrakuraka warlarrakuraka wirlpirla
Waku mirntirrirla waku mirntirrirla wirlpirla
Waku mirntirrirla waku mirntirrirla wirlpirla

♩=160

Line A: Wa ku mirn ti rri rla   wa ku mirn ti rri rla   wirl pi rla
Line B: Wa rlu ra   ku ra ka   wa rlu ra   ku ra ka   wirl pi rla

*See also Verse 49 in Curran (2020: 170).

The women are dancing, holding their arms loosely out in front of themselves to dance, with fast movements.

---

waku: arm.
waku mirntirri: holding their arms out in front of themselves to dance, with arms and hands loose and swinging. They are looking around and bending low as they dance.
wirlpirla: quick.
warlarrakurakurla: quick, loose, moving their arms quickly; a little bit like quivering.

Perentie eggs.
Photo by Suzanne Bryce 1982 © Ara Iritija archive AI-0027346-001

20. Warakija

Warakija
Warakija
Ngipiri ngarnungarnu
Ngipiri ngarnungarnu

Line A: Wu ra ki ja

Line B: Nga pi ri nga rnu nga rnu

*See also Verse 33 in Curran (2020: 162).

The women wanted some eggs, and they were moving around looking for them. They found some eggs from goannas, emus or bush turkeys in a place called Ngipiri.

ngarnu ngarnu: "I'm already eating this one, this egg."
ngarnungarnu: also interpreted as highly desirable, highly prized, *Warlpiri Encyclopaedic Dictionary*.
ngipiri: egg. It also refers to a place.
wara: "Ah yeah, look! I've got everything here that I need."

Henry Cooke Jakamarra singing Yuupurnju, Lajamanu, NT.
Image from recordings of the song cycle, 2013.

21. Waku jumpurujumpuru

Waku jumpuru-jumpuru
Waku jumpuru karrinya

Line A: Wa ku jum pu ru   jum pu ru
Line B: Wa ku jum pu ru   ka rri nya

The women are dancing, holding their arms out.

---

karri: standing up together, dancing.

waku jumpuru-jumpuru: the women are holding their arms out at waist and chest height, with their arms in a kind of circle, moving them just a little bit.

waku: arm.

Water in desert bloodwood bowl.
© Fiona Walsh 2023

22. Yalurrpalurrpungulu

Yanulpanulpungulu nyinanjarlarra parra
Yanulpanulpungulu nyinanjarlarra parra
Wangarlanjirri-ngirli nyinanjarlarra parra
Wangarlanjirri-ngirli nyinanjarlarra parra

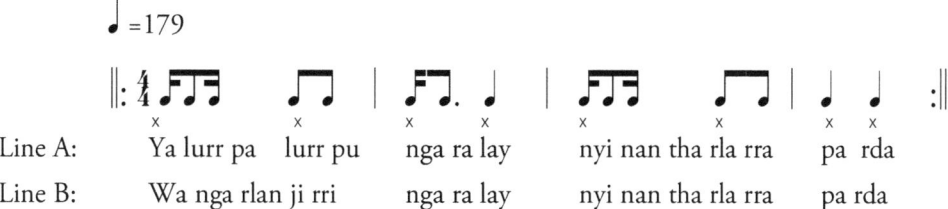

Line A: Ya lurr pa lurr pu | nga ra lay | nyi nan tha rla rra | pa rda
Line B: Wa nga rlan ji rri | nga ra lay | nyi nan tha rla rra | pa rda

A crow is sitting down, and the women come along and find the crow sitting there, drinking water. This is at Wangarla Bore, near Yarrungkanyi.

nyinanjarlarra: each one is sitting, drinking water.

parra: daytime; they are sitting during the day.

wangarla: crow; another word for crow is *kaarnka*.

wangarlanjirri-ngirli: crow. The crow stole and drank water from the coolamon.

yanulpanulpungulu: coolamon, a shallow wooden dish for carrying water. A spoken Warlpiri word for this is *mardu*.

yanurrpu: a large wooden bowl, especially used for carrying water, *Warlpiri Encyclopaedic Dictionary*.

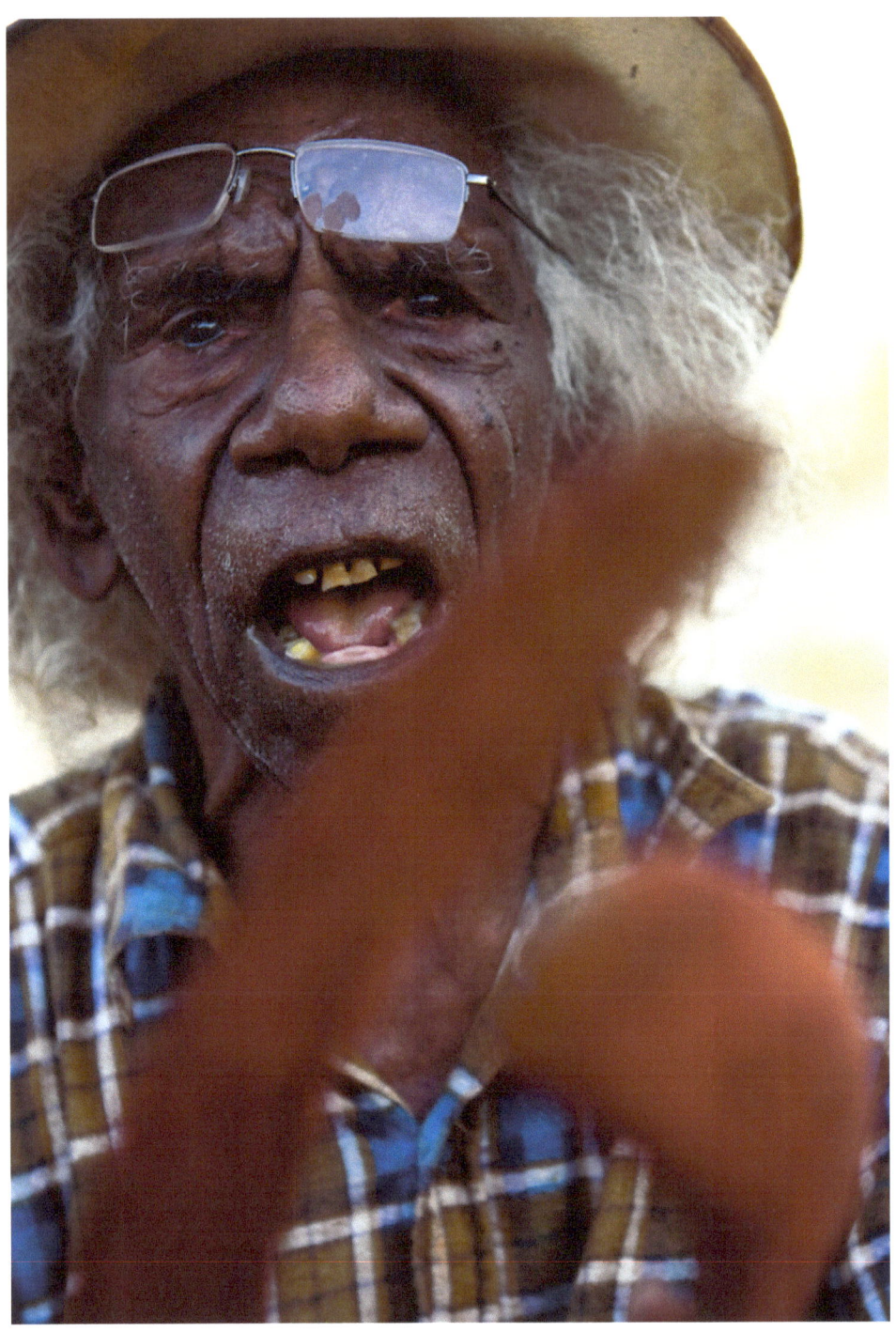

Henry Cooke Jakamarra, Lajamanu, NT.
© Peter Eve, courtesy Tracks Dance Company

23. Yarlangki

Yarlarnki jalangka jalangka
Yujuyuju panturnu
Yujuyuju panturnu

Line A: Ya rlang ki   ja lang ka   jalang kay

Line B: Yul ja yul   jay   pan tu rna

Now the women are dancing, using the digging sticks.

> *jalangka*: here, or today, now; *jalangu* in spoken Warlpiri.
>
> *panturnu*: moving, dancing, touching something. In this verse, its interpretation is tapping the sticks on the ground.
>
> *yarlarnki jalangka*: the women pick up the digging sticks, standing them up, using them like tapping them, upright, into the ground.
>
> *Yarlarnkirri*: a place name.
>
> *yujuyuju*: using the sticks down on the ground, standing them up, tapping them on the ground while dancing.

Yinirnti – red and yellow seeds from the bean tree (*Erythrina vespertilio*).
© Fiona Walsh 2018

24. Yinirnti

Yinirnti namparri namparrina ya
Yinirnti namparri namparrina ya
Yinirnti jilypirri jilypirri ya
Yinirnti jilypirri jilypirri ya

Line A: Yi ni rnti nam pa rri nam pa rri na ya

Line B: Yi nirn ti jily pay jily pay ya

*See also Verse 38 in Curran (2020: 164).

The women have cupped hands, holding yinirnti seeds from the bean tree. They put the beans on their necks or on their heads, as decorations. Sometimes they have the yinirnti in their hands, shaking them to make a rattling noise during the dance. The words are the action of putting them on. (In a present-day performance of dancing to this verse, sometimes the women put the beans in a container and shake it during their dance.)

> *jilypirri jilypirrina*: the women have the beans in their hands.
> *jilypirrimi*: fill up, fill to capacity, *Warlpiri Encyclopaedic Dictionary*.
> *namparri*: picking up *yinirnti* seeds that have fallen from the tree.

Fruit of one of the different types of bush tomatoes (*Solanum chippendalei*). Warlpiri recognise a variety of different species, and use different names for the stages of processing, including *ngayaki*, *kurla-parnta*, *nganjawarli*.
© Fiona Walsh 1986

25. Warnamarra

Warnamarra jitijiti
Ngapaly-ngapaly parnkayarra

♩.=80

| Line A: | Wa rna ma rra ji di | ji di |
| Line B: | Nga pa nga paly parn ka | ya rra |

*Sometimes at the last syllable of the lines, the short note is left off.

The women find bush tomatoes to eat.

> *jitijiti*: the seeds.
>
> *ngapaly-ngapaly parnkayarra*: bush tomatoes and trees growing up everywhere, partly on top of each other, overlapping each other, in a clump.
>
> *warnamarra*: the bush tomatoes grow on vines in straight lines.
>
> *ngayaki*, *kurla-parnta*, *nganjawarli* are also words for bush tomato (*Solanum chippendalei*), *Warlpiri Encyclopaedic Dictionary*.

Hot coals of a mulga fire.
© Fiona Walsh 2019

26. Jurdurrungkarni

Jurdurrungkarni jangi jurdurrungkarni

♩.=82

Line A: Ju rdu rrung ka rni

Line B: Ja ki ju rdu rrung ka rni

*In the last iteration of the verse, *jangi* is replaced with *ngiji*. Singers can use either word. See also Verse 27 in Curran (2020: 158).

The women dance in the area near a fire. When they finish dancing, they cover up the fire with dirt so that it goes out.

> *jangi*: fire stick, or red-hot coals, also called *ngiji*. When sung, it can sound like *jaki*.
>
> *jurdurrungkarni*: related to *jurdurr-yinyi* "cover with, pile on top of (typically earth, ash, coals)", *Warlpiri Encyclopaedic Dictionary*. Jangala explains that in the song this word means "when they finish with the fire, when they finish dancing, they cover up the fire with dirt so that it goes out".

Emus walking.
© Bob McDougall 2019

27. Jipily jipily

Jipily jipily parrayana
Walangkarna kaninjarra

♩=145

Line A: Ji pily ji pily pa rra ya na
Line B: Wa lang ka rna ka nin ja rra

*Sometimes at the last syllable of the lines, the short note is left off.

The women see an emu walking and sing about it.

> *jipily jipily parrayana*: the emu is lifting its legs up while it's walking.
> *kaninjarra*: down.
> *parrayana*: walking across.
> *yana*: walking in the plains country.
> *walangka*: plains country.

Wulpayi "creek" in flow.
© Carmel O'Shannessy 2021

28. Wulpayi

Wulpayi parnka wulpayi parnka parnka
Wulpayi parnka wulpayi parnka parnka
Rilinji parnka rilinji parnka parnka
Rilinji parnka rilinji parnka parnka

Line A: Wul pa yi   parn ka   wul pa yi   parn ka   parn ka
Line B: Rri lin ji   parn ka   rri lin ji   parn ka   parn ka

Water is running in a creek.

---

parnka parnka: "It's running, the creek is running."
rilinji: the sand in the creek.
wulpayi: creek.

Henry Cooke Jakamarra singing Yuupurnju, Lajamanu, NT.
Image from recordings of the song cycle, 2013.

29. Kurlarda wangardijarrili

Kurlarda wangardijarrili
Yararrararralu manu
Yararrararralu manu

The women pick up the spear from a wind break, a little spear; they drag it along a little bit.

The women travel from Cannon Hill through Kurlungalinypa to Jangalpangalpa in the east. This is sung by the Warnayaka Warlpiri people. (It is not clear if this verse is usually part of this song cycle.)

---

kurlarda: spear.

wangardi: might be a word for spear.

yararrararralu manu: they got it out from a windbreak.

Tracks of red kangaroos hopping.
© Fiona Walsh 2022

30. Wawirrina

Wawirrina parnkulparnka
Yirlimintirrina karri

♩.=85

Line A: Wa wi rri na parn kul parn ka
Line B: Yi rli mi nti rri na ka rri

*See also Verse 17 in Curran (2020: 153).

A kangaroo was bounding along with big jumps. The women see the kangaroo tracks, they see that it had been running there. The kangaroo ran straight up through Purrkiji (the Granites).

karri: standing.
parnkulparnka: the kangaroo ran straight up through Purrkiji (the Granites).
wawirri: kangaroo, eastern Warlpiri word (from Arandic).
yirlimintirrina: two legs, moving higher, running.

Henry Cooke Jakamarra singing Yuupurnju, Lajamanu, NT.
Image from recordings of the song cycle, 2013.

31. Wurnapa ngarrkanta

Wurnapa ngarrkanta ngarrkanta
Wurnapa ngarrkanta ngarrkanta
Wurnapa jurlurlu wirntinya
Wurnapa jurlurlu wirntinya

Line A: Wu rna pa   ngarr kan ta   ngarr kan ta
Line B: Wu rna pa   ji rli rli   wirn ti nya

*Throughout this song, Jakamarra keeps time by beating an empty bottle.

The women are dancing. Their feet slide on the ground in the dance movements. There is dust from their dancing feet.

> *jurlurlu*: dust from the ground on the dancers' feet. Their feet are sliding a little bit as they dance.
>
> *wirntinya*: dancing, typically dancing by women. A way to say "dancing", called the presentative form, common in traditional songs.
>
> *wurna*: walking, travelling.

Jipilyka "pretty flower".
© Carmel O'Shannessy 2014

32. Ngati mulyumulyu

Ngati mulyumulyu parntirla parntirla
Ngati mulyumulyu parntirla parntirla
Jipilyka parntirla parntirla parntirla
Jipilyka parntirla parntirla parntirla

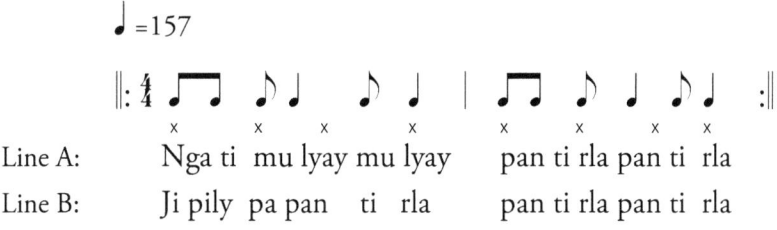

Line A: Nga ti mu lyay mu lyay   pan ti rla pan ti rla
Line B: Ji pily pa pan   ti   rla   pan ti rla pan ti rla

A mother is smelling something, a pretty flower from a tree.

---

jipilyka: pretty flower; *jinjirla* in spoken Warlpiri.
mulyumulyu: nose; *mulyu* in spoken Warlpiri.
ngati: mother.
parnti-: to smell.

Rain in the distance, Tanami Desert.
© Carmel O'Shannessy 2022

33. Ngapakurla

Ngapa kurla yinirnti pirlkiri ngunanya
Ngapa kurla yinirnti pirlkiri ngunanya
Ngapa kurlayi jurardi jurardi ngunanya
Ngapa kurlayi jurardi jurardi ngunanya

Line A: Nga pa ku rla yi nirn ti   pirl ki ri ngu nan tha

Line B: Nga pa ku rla ju ra rdi   ju ra rdi ngu nan tha

*See also Verse 46 in Curran (2020: 168).

The women come across rain. The water from the rain is running on the ground.

> *jurrardi jurrardi ngunanya*: in the creek, when the creek is flowing.
> *ngapa*: rain.
> *wardirnti pirlkirring*: the women come across some rain that is running on the ground, or, it's raining. (Jangala said: the line should be *walirdi pirlkirring ngunanya*: in a straight line, the rain is running in straight lines on the ground.)

Aerial view of Lake Lewis, Anmatyerr country, NT.
© Peter Carroll

34. Lyinjirrmarlinja

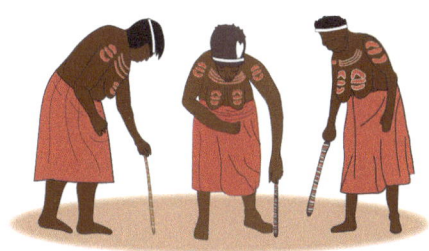

Lyinjarrayarla namarrayarla nami
Lyinjarrayarla namarrayarla nami
Lyinjirrmarlinja linjirrmarlinja limi
Lyinjirrmarlinja linjirrmarlinja limi

Line A: Lyin jirr ma rlin ja lin jirr ma rlin ja li mi
Line B: Lyin ja rra ya rla na ma rra ya rla na mi

Here the people are in Anmatyerr Country. The men are sitting in a place, and the women are dancing. They dance with one leg staying in one place as a pivot, and the other leg moves around, turning their bodies around.

*This song is said to be in Anmatyerr language, because the women are now in Anmatyerr Country.

A desert truffle species (*Elderia arenivaga*) dries to look like a yellow apricot.
© Fiona Walsh 1990

35. Wardijayi

Wardijayi marntulaya limali marntulaya

Line A: Wa rti ja   man tu rla ya
Line B: Li ma li   man tu rla ya

Jangala said that an additional line of this song would be:

Wardijayi marntulaya ngari-wilyi-wilyi.

The women find some food. It appears when cold weather comes, after a rain. Ah, *ngari-wilyi-wilyi* is growing here, in mulga country. One man was called Wilyiri; maybe he was in the Japangardi skin name group.

---

limalima or *lumaluma*: *ngari-wilyi-wilyi* is growing here.

ngari-wilyi-wilyi: new shoots of bush tucker, fungi or mushrooms. These grow on the ground after rain. *Ngari-wilyi-wilyi* looks like a dried apricot, white and yellow.

wardijayi: mulga tree (*Acacia aneura*).

wardiji: mulga in Warlpiri, except in Yuendumu and Nyirrpi communities; also *manja*: mulga in Warlpiri (see Song 10).

wilyiri: an edible fungus, or truffle (*Elderia arenivaga*), *Warlpiri Encyclopaedic Dictionary*.

Footprint in the wind-blown sands over a termite bed.
© Fiona Walsh 2021

36. Junpurla

Junpurlarula wuma
Parlanji wirrayi-wirrayi

Line A:	Jin pi rla	ri la		wu ma	
Line B:	Pi rlan ji	wi rray		wi rray	

*See also Verse 7 in Curran (2020: 148).

The women are dancing on the flat termite bed; they leave marks there on the earth.

> *junpurla*: the disturbance on the earth from the women's dancing.
>
> *parlanji*: a termite bed that is relatively flat, raised above the surrounding ground. This area is a really flat and clear place to dance, a good place to dance, on the flat termite beds (see also Song 13).
>
> *wirrayi-wirrayi*: the women are dancing on the termite bed, they leave marks there on the earth.
>
> *wuma*: the movement of the dancers.

Henry Cooke Jakamarra singing Yuupurnju, Lajamanu, NT.
Image from recordings of the song cycle, 2013.

37. Yirarri-rarri-manu

Yirarri-rarri-manu
Yirarri-rarri-manu
Yalarnkalarnkardijarrarla

The women are aware of how they have always danced. They are celebrating as they are spinning in the dance, and getting tired from it.

Yalarnkalarnkardijarrarla: this has always been done this way. The women know they will get dizzy from spinning as they dance, but they are also celebrating.

Yirarri-rarri-manu: the women are dancing with the digging sticks, turning around and around, and getting exhausted, spinning from all the exercise, on the dancing ground.

Henry Cooke Jakamarra painting a shield, Lajamanu, NT.
© Ludo Kuipers 1976

38. Pinapi-rnalu

Pinapi-rnalu yilkiki-yirrarnu
Pinapi-rnalu yilkiki-yirrarnu
Kanali yilkiki-yirrarnu
Kanali yilkiki-yirrarnu

Line A: Pi na pi na li   yirr ki ki   yi rra rnu

Line B: Ka rna li   yirr ki ki   yi rra rnu

The women hold the digging sticks as a support when they're dancing in a circle, dancing all over the dance area. They bring their knees together as a dance movement.

kana: the digging sticks; the women hold the digging sticks as a support when they're dancing in a circle, dancing all over the dance area.

pinapi: when the women are dancing, they bring their knees together; you can hear the sounds of the legs clapping in contact with each other. From *pinapina*, to make contact.

yirrarnu: "do-past": to have done something, in spoken Warlpiri.

Henry Cooke Jakamarra carving, Lajamanu, NT.
© Ludo Kuipers 1976

Henry Cooke Jakamarra spinning hair string, Lajamanu, NT.
© Ludo Kuipers 1976

References

Curran, Georgia (2010). Contemporary ritual practice in an Aboriginal settlement: The Warlpiri Kurdiji ceremony. PhD thesis, School of Archaeology and Anthropology, Australian National University, Canberra. https://openresearch-repository.anu.edu.au/handle/1885/9784.

Curran, Georgia (2020). *Sustaining Indigenous Songs: Contemporary Warlpiri Ceremonial Life in Central Australia*. New York, Oxford: Berghahn Books.

Curran, Georgia (ed.) (2017). *Yurntumu-wardingki juju-ngaliya-kurlangu yawulyu: Warlpiri Women's Songs from Yuendumu* [including DVD]. Batchelor: Batchelor Institute Press.

Dobson, Veronica (2007). *Arelhe-kenhe merrethene: Arrernte Traditional Healing*. Alice Springs: IAD Press.

Dussart, Françoise (2000). *The Politics of Ritual in an Aboriginal Settlement: Kinship, Gender and the Currency of Knowledge*. Washington, London: The Smithsonian Institution Press.

Gallagher, Coral Napangardi, Peggy Nampijinpa Brown, Georgia Curran and Barbara Napanangka Martin (2014). *Jardiwanpa yawulyu: Warlpiri Women's Songs from Yuendumu*. Batchelor: Batchelor Institute Press.

Green, Jennifer (2008). *Eastern and Central Anmatyerr to English Dictionary*. Alice Springs, NT: IAD Press.

Japanangka, Maxwell Walma Tasman and Carmel O'Shannessy (2020). *Kaja-warnu-jangka* "From the Bush". Film. Yuendumu: Pintupi Anmatyerr Warlpiri Media and Communications (PAW Media). https://bit.ly/4b2EKCE.

Laughren, Mary, Georgia Curran, Myfany Turpin and Nicolas Peterson (2016). "Women's *Yawulyu* Songs as Evidence of Connections to and Knowledge of Land: The Jardiwanpa". In *Language, Land and Song: Studies in Honour of Luise Hercus*, edited by Peter K. Austin, Harold Koch and Jane Simpson, 419–50. London: EL Publishing.

Laughren, Mary, Kenneth Hale, Jeannie Egan Nungarrayi, Marlurrku Paddy Patrick Jangala, Robert Hoogenraad, David Nash and Jane Simpson (2022). *Warlpiri Encyclopaedic Dictionary*. Canberra: Aboriginal Studies Press.

Meggitt, Mervyn (1962). *Desert People*. Sydney: Angus & Robertson.

Nicholls, Christine Judith (2014). "Dreamtime" and "The Dreaming" – an introduction. *The Conversation*, 23 January 2014. https://bit.ly/3O8mfT8.

Stanner, W.E.H. (1979) *White man got no dreaming: Essays 1938–1973*. Canberra: Australian National University Press.

Turpin, Myfany (2007). The poetics of Central Australian song. *Australian Aboriginal Studies* 2: 100–15.

Turpin, Myfany (2022). End rhyme in Aboriginal sung poetry. In *Rhyme and Rhyming in Verbal Art, Language, and Song*, edited by Nigel Fabb and Venla Sykari, 212–27. Studia Fennica Folkloristica 25. Helsinki: Finnish Literature Society. https://doi.org/10.21435/sff.25.

Turpin, Myfany and Lana Henderson (2015). Tools for analysing verbal art in the field. *Language Documentation and Conservation* 9: 89–109.

Wild, Stephen A. (1975). Walbiri music and dance in their social and cultural nexus. PhD thesis, Indiana University, Bloomington, Indiana.

Appendix 1: Correspondences between verses in the Yuupurnju and *Karntakarnta* song cycles

Some verses with the same or similar words also occur in a similar song cycle performed in Yuendumu in 2007, taking a more southern route (Curran 2020). The correspondences are indicated on each page of this book as they occur, and given here.

Table 1.1. Yuupurnju verses that were also sung in the *Karntakarnta* song cycle as documented in Curran 2020

Yuupurnju verse	Corresponding verse number and page in Curran 2020
1 Kanaku kanakurla	---
2 Karrinjapardi	---
3 Tangkirrina	---
4 Wujuju-wangkanya	#18 p154
5 Yajankurlarri	#16 p153
6 Yanganpa	---
7 Yarrintirlarnu	---
8 Jinapi	---
9 Miyinmarrirla	---
10 Manja kurrkurrku	---
11 Jujuju japarnti	---
12 Walangkaju	#2 p145
13 Palararrararra	#8 p149
14 Kartiwirntinya	---
15 Warrawarra	---

Yuupurnju verse	Corresponding verse number and page in Curran 2020
16 Yuluwurru	#48 p169
17 Yangipi yantakuyanta	---
18 Karnta wurrparna	#29 p160
19 Waku mirntirrirla	#49 p170
20 Warakija	#33 p162
21 Waku jumpurujumpuru	---
22 Yalurrpalurrpungulu	---
23 Yarlangki	---
24 Yinirnti	#38 p164
25 Warnamarra	---
26 Jurdurrungkarni	#27 p158
27 Jipily jipily	---
28 Wulpayi	---
29 Kurlarda wangardijarrili	---
30 Wawirrina	#17 p153
31 Wurnapa ngarrkanta	---
32 Ngati mulyumulyu	---
33 Ngapakurla	#46 p168
34 Lyinjirrmarlinja	---
35 Wardijayi	---
36 Junpurla	#7 p148
37 Yirarri-rarri-manu	---
38 Pinapi-rnalu	---

Appendix 2: Sequence of verses on the recordings

Jakamarra sang the 38 verses presented in this book across 12 days. Mostly these were sequential days, except for Days 3 and 4; and 8 and 9 where there was a break of one and then two days respectively. Most days consisted of multiple recordings, as the recording was stopped for various reasons. For example, when Jakamarra broke for lunch, or a visitor stopped by, or the batteries in the recorder needed changing. Two recordings did not contain any singing, only talking (HenryCooke08132013_5 and HenryCooke08212013_4), so we have not listed these in the table below.

In performance, a verse is typically sung multiple times before moving on to the next verse. This is a feature of all central Australian ceremonial singing; and in some languages it is described as "spreading out the verse" (Turpin and Henderson 2015: 97). For example, on Day 1 Jakamarra began with Verse 1 sung twice, followed by Verse 2 sung twice. On later days, a verse was sometimes "spread out" up to 12 times. Musicologists often describe the multiple spreading out of a verse as "song items". Song items have a particular melodic structure, ending on a low, quiet note. In total, Jakamarra sang 1,335 song items. Song items can be interspersed with "talking" on the pitch of the melody, an intoned speech style, which does not interrupt the melodic structure of the song item. The division into song items, however, is not always clear cut, as sometimes a song doesn't complete the entire melodic structure.

In the performance of Yuupurnju, Jakamarra often returns to the same verse later on. It is not clear if there is a significance behind the return to a verse. Perhaps the verse accompanies a recurring dance, or a recurring theme, such as when a protagonist is travelling. Some verses that recur frequently across the 12 days are Verses 8 and 13. While there does not appear to be any set order of the verses, some verses come as "pairs"; for example, Verses 13 and 14 and Verses 15 and 16.

In the table, the first column lists each of the 12 days that Jakamarra sang. The second column provides the archival file name of the recording. The third column lists the verses in the sequence they were sung, while the fourth column is the total number of song items sung on the recording.

The asterisks in the third column represent a verse from a different song series. On occasion, Jakamarra starts singing one verse but switches to another verse mid-singing. This is represented by '/'. For example, on Day 7, in the first recording he began to sing Verse 21 and then it became Verse 13.

Table 1.2. Sequence of songs on the recordings

Day	Recording	Verse identification number (numbered songs in this book)	No. song items
1	HC08082013_1	1, 1, 2, 2, 1, 2, 2, 2, 2, 1, 3, 3, 3, 3, 4, 4, 5, 5, 1, 2, 2, 2, 2, 6, 6, 6, 6, 6.	30
	HC08082013_2	6, 8, 9, 10, 10, 7, 7, 7, 7, 10, 10, 7, 7, 7, 6, 7, 10, 10, 7, 10, 5, 5.	24
2	HC08092013_1	1, 1, 2, 2, 1, 12, 12, 13, 13, 14, 8, 8, 8, 8, 4, 4, 5, 5, 5, 5, 5, 5, 8, 8, 15, 15, 16, 16, 15, 15, 17, 17, 17, 17, 9, 9, 12.	41
	HC08092013_2	17, 17, 17, 12, 12, 13, 13, 13, 13, 3, 22, 22, 22, 22, 22.	16
3	HC08102013_1	18, 18, 18, 18, 18, 19, 19, 19.	9
	HC08102013_2	2, 2, 2, 2, 2, 3, 3, 20, 20, 16, 16, 15, 15, 13, 13, 13, 13, 21, 21, 21, 13, 4, 4, 4, 8, 13, 13, 13, 13, 22, 22, 22, 22, 22, 22.	35
	HC08102013_3	22, 23, 23, 23, 10, 10, 10, 10, 10, 7, 7, 5, 5, 10, 10, 10, 10, 5, 5, 8, 8, 8, 13, 13, 13.	27
	HC08102013_4	3, 3, 24, 1, 1, 10, 10, 13, 13, 13, 13, 10, 10, 13, 13, 23, 23, 23, 6, 6, 6, 6, 6, 6, 13, 13.	30
	HC08102013_5	13, 8, 8, 8.	4
4	HC08122013_1	1, 1, 2, 2, 2, 2, 1, 1, 2, 2, 13, 13, 13, 13, 13, 13, 12, 12, 25, 25, 25, 10, 10, 10, 10, 10, 8.	31
	HC08122013_2	8, 8, 8, 8, 8, 8, 25, 6, 6, 13, 13, 13, 13, 26, 26, 26, 26, 8, 8, 13, 13, 23, 23.	28
	HC08122013_3	23, 23, 4, 4, 4, 4, 5, 5, 5, 5, 22, 22, 23, 23, 10, 10, 8, 8, 8, 8, 8, 2, 2.	29
	HC08122013_4	8, 8, 8, 8, 8, 12, 25, 25, 25, 8, 8, 2, 2, 2, 2, 13, 13, 13, 13, 14, 14, 14, 18, 18, 18, 4, 8, 8.	33
	HC08122013_5	12, 12, 27, 27, 27, 27, 27, 5, 5, 5, 10, 10, 8, 8, 8, 12.	17
5	HC08132013_1	28, 28, 28, 28, 29, 29, 29, 20, 20, 29, 3, 3, 3, 3, 3, 3, 13, 13, 13, 13, 14, 14, 14, 14, 10, 10.	30
	HC08132013_2	4, 4, 4, 4, 22, 22, 22, 22, 22, 22.	37
	HC08132013_3	22, 8, 8, 8, 8, 8, 8, 6, 8, 8, 8, 8, 23, 23, 23, 23, 23, 23, 8, 8, 8, 8, 10, 6, 6, 6, 6, 6, 31, 31, 31.	31
	HC08132013_4	18, 18, 18, 18, 8, 8, 8, 13, 13, 13.	11

Day	Recording	Verse identification number (numbered songs in this book)	No. song items
6	HC08142013_1	27, 27, 27, 12, 12, 12, 27, 27, 27, 13, 13, 13, 8, 8, 8, 8, 8, 8, 8, 8, 27, 27, 27, 27.	35
	HC08142013_2	8, 8, 33, 33, 13, 13, 13, 13, 13, 13, 13, 4, 4, 4, 4, 13, 13, 13, 13, 13, 13.	38
7	HC08152013_1	21, 21, 21, 21, 21, 21/13, 21, 28, 28, 28, 20, 20, 20, 20.	19
	HC08152013_2	28, 28, 28/20, 29, 29, 29, 29, 29, 29, 29, 20, 29, 29, 6, 6, 6, 28, 6, 6, 6.	25
	HC08152013_3	6, 6, 6, 6, 10, 10, 10, 22, 22, 22, 22, 22, 22, 22, 22, *, *, 22, 22.	23
8	HC08162013_1	29, 29, 29, 29, 29, 29, 28, 28.	9
	HC08162013_2	28.	1
	HC08162013_3	28, 28, 28, 28, 28, 20, 20, 20, 23, 23, 23, 23, 23, 23, 37, 37, 36, 36, 36, 36, 37, 37, 37.	27
	HC08162013_4	37, 21, 21, 21, 21, 21, 21, 21, 13, 13, 13, 13, 13, 13, 13, 13, 13, 13, 13, 8, 8, 8, 8, 8.	30
	HC08162013_5	8, 15, 15, 15, 15, 15, 15, 16, 16, 15, 30, 30, 30, 30, 8.	16
9	HC08192013_1	17, 17, 17, 17, 17, 17, 17, 2, 2, 2, 2, 2, 2, 2, 2, 1, 1, 1, 1, 1, 13, 13, 13, 13, 13, 13, 13, 13, 14, 14.	38
	HC08192013_2	14, 14, 14, 34, 34, 34, 34, 34, 34, 34, 8, 8, 8, 8, 25, 25, 25.	20
	HC08192013_3	5, 5, 5, 5, 5, 5, 5, 5, 5, 27, 27, 27, 27, 27, 27, 3, 3, 3, 3, 3, 8, 8, 8, 8, 8, 8, 8, 4, 4, 4, 4, 4, 4, 4, 4.	36
	HC08192013_4	4, 4, 13, 13, 13, 13, 13, 14, 3, 3, 3, 3, 3, 3, 3, 3, 3, 3, 8, 8, 8, 8, 8, 13, 13, 13, 13, 13, 13, 13.	32
	HC08192013_5	13, 13, 13, 18, 18, 18, 18, 18, 18, 18, 18, 1, 1, 1, 1, 35, 2, 2, 2, 2, 2, 2, 1.	26
	HC08192013_6	1, 1, 1, 2, 2, 2, 2, 2, 13, 13, 13, 13, 13, 13.	15
	HC08192013_7	13, 13, 13, 13, 13, 13, 31, 31, 31, 31, 31, 31, 3, 3, 3, 3, 3, 26, 26, 26, 26, 26, 26, 26, 26, 26, 26, 26, 26, 23, 23, 23, 23, 23, 23, 38, 38, 2, 2, 2, 2.	47
	HC08192013_8	2.	1
	HC08192013_9	4, 4, 4, 4, 4, 4, 4, 4, 28, 28, 28, 28, 20, 20, 20, 20, 29, 29, 29, 29, 29, 29, 29.	24

Day	Recording	Verse identification number (numbered songs in this book)	No. song items
10	HC08202013_1	34, 34, 34, 34, 34, 34.	6
	HC08202013_2	34, 34, 34, 34, 34, 15, 15, 15, 15, 15, 15, 15, 15, 15, 15, 33, 33, 33, 33, 33, 13, 13, 13, 13, 13, 13, 13, 13, 13, 13, 13, 14.	35
	HC08202013_3	14, 14, 14, 13, 13, 13, 13, 13, 14, 18, 18, 18, 18, 18, 18, 18, 18, 19, 19.	20
	HC08202013_4	19, 19, 19, 19, 19, 19, 19, 19, 19, 18, 18, 18, 18, 18, 13, 13, 13, 13, 13, 13, 13, 13, 13, 13, 6, 6, 6, 6, 6, 6, 6, 6, 6, 6, 3, 3, 3.	40
	HC08202013_5	3, 13, 13, 13, 13, 13, 13, 13, 13, 13, 13, 2, 2, 2, 18, 18, 18, 18, 18, 18, 18, 18, 14, 14, 14, 18, 18, 18, 18, 18, 18, 18, 18, 18, 18, 18, 18, 18.	38
	HC08202013_6	18, 18, 19, 19, 19, 19, 19, 19, 18.	9
11	HC08212013_1	27, 27, 27, 27, 27, 27, 27, 27, 8, 8, 8, 8, 8, 8, 8, 30, 30, 30, 30, 30, 10, 13, 13, 13, 13, 13, 13, 13, 13, 13, 13, 13, 13.	33
	HC08212013_2	13, 13, 25, 25, 25, 25, 25, 25, 25, 25, 28, 28, 28, 28, 28, 28, 20, 20, 20, 20, 29, 29, 29, 29, 29, 29, 3, 3, 3, 3, 3, 13, 13, 13, 13, 13, 13.	38
	HC08212013_3	13, 8, 8, 8, 8, 10, 10, 10, 10, 10, 8, 8, 8.	15
	HC08212013_5	8, 8, 8, 8, 8, 8, 8, 8, 25, 25, 25, 12, 12, 12, 25, 25, 8, 8, 9, 9, 10, 10, 10, 10, 10, 10, 10, 10, 15, 15, 15, 15, 15/30, 15, 15, 15, 30, 30, 30.	44
	HC08212013_6	20, 20, 20, 20, 20, 34, 34, 34, 34, 34, 27, 27, 27, 27, 27, 27, 27, 27, 28, 28, 28, 28, 13, 13, 13, 13, 13, 14, 14, 14, 14, 18, 18, 18, 18.	45
	HC08212013_7	27, 27, 27, 27, 27, 27, 25, 25, 13, 13, 13, 13, 13, 13, 13, 13, 13, 13, 13.	21
12	HC08222013_1	29, 29, 29, 29, 29, 29, 29, 29, 29, 28, 28, 28, 28, 28, 28, 28, 28, 28, 28, 20, 20, 20, 20, 20, 20, 20, 20.	36
	HC08222013_2	13, 13, 13, 13, 13, 13, 13, 13, 13, 13, 13, 13, 13, 13, 15, 15, 15, 15, 16, 16, 16, 16, 16, 16, 16, 16, 16, 16.	30
	Total number of song items		1335

www.ingramcontent.com/pod-product-compliance
Lightning Source LLC
Chambersburg PA
CBHW041127300426
44113CB00003B/89